The Writer's Guide to

WRITING YOUR YOUR SCREENPLAY

The Writer's Guide to

WRITING YOUR SCREENPLAY

How to Write Great Screenplays for Movies and Television

BY CYNTHIA WHITCOMB

The Writer Books

The Writer Books is an imprint of Kalmbach Trade Press, a division of Kalmbach Publishing Co. These books are distributed to the book trade by Watson-Guptill.

For all other inquiries, including individual orders or details on special quantity discounts for groups or conferences, contact:

Kalmbach Publishing Co.
21027 Crossroads Circle
Waukesha, WI 53187
(800) 533-6644

Visit our website at http://writermag.com
Secure online ordering available

Printed in Canada

02 03 04 05 06 07 08 09 10 11   10 9 8 7 6 5 4 3 2 1

Publisher's Cataloging-in-Publication

Whitcomb, Cynthia.
    The writer's guide to writing your screenplay : how
to write great screenplays for movies and television /
by Cynthia Whitcomb. — 1st ed.
    p. cm.
    Includes bibliographical references and index.
    ISBN: 0-87116-191-5

    1. Motion picture authorship. 2. Television
authorship. 3. Motion pictures—Vocational guidance.
4. Television—Vocational guidance. I. Title.
II. Title: Writing your screenplay

    PN1996.W45 2002   808.2'3
                                QBI02-701017

Art Director: Kristi Ludwig
Page Layout: Linda Wenzel

Author photo on back cover is by Molly Mandelberg.

This book is dedicated to my children.

Table of Contents

Preface

As a child, I grew up in a family where both my grandfathers were Nazarene preachers. Movies were considered a sin. I didn't step over the line into the dark and sinful interior of a theater to see my first movie until I was 16. That first movie was *The Sound of Music*. From the opening panoramic shot of the Alps, I fell in love with movies and have never looked back. By age 17, I was working nights after high school at a theater selling popcorn—and sneaking in to watch every movie. By age 18, I was at UCLA Film School catching up on all the great movies I had missed: Hitchcock, Lubitsch, Lean, Scorsese, all the greats. My love affair with movies is still going strong.

I wrote ten feature-length spec scripts before I sold anything, so I'm a good example of breaking in the hard way. Many of my students have begun to sell their screenplays after writing only two or three scripts—so, with guidance, things can happen more quickly for you than it did for me.

Over my career, I have sold (or been hired to write) 70 screenplays (13 feature films, 42 movies for television, and 14 TV miniseries), of which 25 have been produced.

Ten years ago, I moved out of California and now live with my family in Oregon. And I have sold more scripts and made more money writing in this location than I did when I lived in L.A.

Speaking from experience, I know about success in this field, and about living in the real world while working for Hollywood. It's possible. You can do it.

As much as ever, I still love movies, love writing, love teaching, and love life.

I hope that this book will be one that writers will pass on to each other. Because it contains what you are really looking for:

Proof that your dreams can come true.

And a lamp that lights the path ahead.

What You Will Learn in This Book

All **who write** have first-hand experience with the duality of the writer's mind. One side (the Right Brain) is the creative, childlike, magical mind. The other side, the Left Brain, is more analytical; it is good at organizing, structuring, researching, proofreading, handling the technical aspects of the craft. Unfortunately it is also prone to criticizing everything the Right Brain is trying to do. The Left Brain is a world-class control freak.

No matter how different they are, these two halves of the brain must work together to write a screenplay. Neither can do it alone. A movie written entirely by the Right Brain would be strange, unstructured, and bizarre. Good movies need structure and a story and characters. They can be wildly original in style, but without these basic elements, they will be awful by nearly everyone's standards.

On the other hand, a movie made entirely by the Left Brain will be heartless and soulless, one of those cookie-cutter clones of some previous hit cranked out by studio assembly lines. These are equally awful. I know some of you are thinking: Yes, but somebody gets paid a lot of money to turn out that junk. Why not me? The reason: They already have people to do that. That job has already been filled. The only way to break into the screenwriting business is to write a terrific, original screenplay. Which is what this book is about.

Both halves of the brain are required to write a great movie. They need to work together and support each other. Their individual contributions need to be protected and valued.

This book presents a method I have developed to teach screenwriting that embraces both Left and Right Brains, using the best of both. I have taught screenwriting for nearly 20 years, seven of those at UCLA Film

School. My students have gone on to earn millions of dollars for their screenplays; some of those were written as class projects. My system is simple. It uses both hemispheres of the brain, sequentially, so they are not fighting with each other. If it were a game like football, it would be like bringing in the Offensive Lineup when you've got the ball, and switching to the Defensive Lineup when you don't. If you try to involve both sides at once, putting all your players on the field, your own team ends up beating itself up.

Here's a synopsis of how the screenwriting game is played.

First, find an idea that you love. Obviously, this initial inspiration is a function of the creative Right Brain. Once it has given you an idea for a movie—and you love it enough that you want to write a screenplay—we're ready to turn it into a successful script.

Part One: The Spine. The Left Brain steps in and goes to work. This process includes reviewing a list of criteria to make sure the idea is strong enough to carry a whole movie. Then you have to research the script, structure it, make scene cards, lay out a storyboard, weave in subplots, and so on. Once that groundwork has been laid, you're ready to write the actual script.

Part Two: The Heart. The Right Brain takes over now. It's time to see the movie in your mind. This is when you write the first draft. It's time for magic to happen. At its best, this part is visual, surprising, and emotional. In this section of the book, you'll find tools to support this right-brain process.

Part Three: The Mind. Now that the magical first draft is done, it's time for the Left Brain to march back onto the field and polish it up. This section is about getting it lean and clean and ready for the marketplace.

Part Four: The Spirit. This is the last step: checking back in with your deepest self. Address once again the theme, and the truth. What are you really saying? What impact will your movie have on the world? This section of the book also deals with setting up important support systems for your-self as a writer.

The four parts of the screenwriting process are all equally important. All are vital for the success of the script: The Spine, The Heart, The Mind, and The Spirit. All four must be present and in balance with each other for the screenplay to live and flourish. Naturally, most of us are better at one aspect than another. This book can help you shine a light into any blind spots you may have, discover any weaknesses, and help you overcome them and turn them into strengths.

This book will give you an overview of the process of screenwriting in all its dimensions:

Structural *and* emotional.

Practical *and* magical.

PART ONE

The Spine

When a story comes to you, wanting to be told, you gather the bones and begin to fit them together to see what sort of skeleton they form and what sort of living creature might develop from them. These bones—the basic building blocks—include characters, story, conflict, setting, and scenes. Shaping them into a solid framework is primarily a Left Brain process; hopefully it is a process in which your love for your project will flourish as well.

This first part of the screenwriting process, creating "The Spine," includes looking at the basic three-act structure, act breaks, and turning points. We will learn how to make scene cards and how to lay out a story-board, and all the details of screenplay format. By the end of this first section of the book, you'll be ready to turn the writing over to the Right Brain, so that magic can happen.

So roll up your sleeves, put your thinking cap on, and let's get to work. Let's build The Spine, beginning with the first vertebra: the idea.

CHAPTER 1

Ideas: Choosing Your Screen Story

What are the basic ingredients that make a great script, and thence a great film? Before you invest weeks in structuring and writing a script, it's wise to step back and run through this basic list of criteria to see if the story holds up. Will it play? Will it hook an audience and keep it on the line until the final fade? They are questions that need to be addressed before you begin writing your screenplay.

They are a screenwriter's checklist, not too far afield from the journalist's "Who, What, When, Where, How, and Why."

The Screen Story Checklist

☑ **Is my central character active?** Someone an audience can relate to and identify with? Is he (or she) sympathetic? Driven? What does he want and how badly? A passive protagonist can be a big problem. In fact, he can sink an otherwise good script. Find ways to make your main character an integral part of the story, not merely an observer. An active protagonist makes things happen, he doesn't just have things happen to him.

The Big Lebowski by the Coen brothers is one example of a passive protagonist killing a film's energy. He's one of those laid-back surfer/stoner/slacker dudes (pick your era) whose primary response to any event is "Far out." Even a strong actor like Jeff Bridges can't help him out of the pit of passivity. This guy could be a great, funny secondary character, like a best friend or sidekick, but if he has to carry the film, it's going to end up lying there on the chaise lounge next to him, with the audience nodding off.

For god's sake, make your protagonist grab the wheel and drive the movie! If you're stuck here, ask yourself, what does he want? How badly? And what's he willing to do to make it happen?

☑ **What's the problem?** Is there a central conflict strong enough to drive the engine of the film all the way through without losing momentum? What is at stake? Will people care? If the stakes are high (life and death, world threat, lost child) this will take care of itself. If the stakes are more subtle— for example, if the central question is "Will Murray sell out, give up being the eccentric lovable fool he is and become just another pencil pusher?"— it will be harder to get the audience emotionally invested. If you can get the audience to care about the *character* and the character to care about the *problem*, you'll get there.

The problem (or central question) must be in place by page 15 at the latest. Page 10 is better. And page 1 is great. And it must not be solved until the climax of the movie.

☑ **Can this story be told visually?** Is it all "talking heads"? Or can the story be shown rather than told? As you begin to plan the story, think about ways to avoid people talking in cars, over meals, or on telephones (these are "talking heads scenes"). Find more visual ways to stage these interactions. What large set-pieces could it include? A carnival, planetary collision, car chase, scaling Mount Everest? Try to see cinematic possibilities now. Imagine what clips they could choose for the Coming Attractions trailer.

☑ **What are the locations?** Where does the story take place? Does it need to be broken out onto a broader canvas? If it is a prison story, can you find ways to get us out of the cells so the audience can breathe? If it all takes place in a submarine, the close quarters and limited visual stimulus may work to help create the claustrophobic feel you want. Even so, an occasional enemy ship or storm on the surface will open it up and give the audience more to see.

☑ **Is it basically an internal story or can it be externalized?** Novels and plays can be difficult to translate into screenplays because they are often basically internal stories. Movies need to play out visually. If the central problem is purely emotional, for example, and not physical, how will you take the audience on a mental, emotional ride? You can't tell us that Joe is having trouble with relationships. You have to show Joe dating, blowing it, and so on. Movie audiences don't have a lot of patience for long, philosophical discussions. But they'll go anywhere, from Alcatraz to Auschwitz, and deal with any issues you choose, if those issues are translated into visual movie terms. In other words: show them, don't tell them.

☑ **What is the time frame?** How much time does this story cover? Is it compact or does it ramble over years? Is there any way to compress it to add energy to the movie? Almost always, the more tightly you can compress time, the better the script (and film) will move. Having to stop the story and wait while characters sleep for the night, for instance, is tedious.

☑ **When does it take place?** Is it contemporary? Historical? Most movies bought and made today are set in the present day. On the other hand, most of the Best Picture Oscars over the last two decades have gone to period pictures. Either way is fine to go, but if you are going historical, be sure to do your homework and research the period carefully.

☑ **Does it involve another reality?** Science fiction, fantasy, futuristic, or horror? If so, you need to be clear on the reality base and the rules before you begin. For example, in a vampire movie, the rules may be that the vampire:

      a) casts no reflection in mirrors;

      b) needs to drink human blood to survive;

      c) can only be killed by sunlight or a stake in the heart.

You can make your own rules, but then you must follow them.

☑ **Is there an antagonist?** Is he a worthy opponent—strong enough to be a real challenge to your protagonist? Who is he and what is motivating him? For the conflict between the antagonist and protagonist to work well, they should be equally matched in terms of power, intellect, presence/

charisma, and resources at the disposal of each. A weak or stupid opponent saps the game of its energy and fun. A football game won by 50 points is boring. One that is won by one point in the last three seconds is not. Make both sides strong and equally matched for a good game. If one is an underdog, it needs to be the hero. The villain should never be the underdog.

☑ **Is there a love story?** If so, think it through. Make those two people unique individuals, not just standard cardboard figures plugged into the plot. And why do they fall in love? It can't be just because they are played by gorgeous movie stars. It is your job to script their meeting and the development of their relationship with enough freshness and detail that we are hooked by it and become invested in its outcome. Avoid slow-motion montages of strolling on beaches at sunset, flower markets, kissing in rain, and so on. Show us scenes of two real people making a real connection.

☑ **Who are the other characters you need to tell this story?** The protagonist usually needs someone to play off of. Even the strongest, most silent heroes have relationships—whether with a mother, drinking buddy, best friend, or psychologist. Make sure you people your movie with vivid secondary characters.

☑ **What's it all about?** Before you go any further, be clear what the story is really about. What are you saying? "Love prevails"? "Justice can be won, even if it's a tough fight"? "Life sucks"? You need to be clear before you begin, so your story can be clear as you write it. You may not plan to send a message with your movie, but it will send one anyway. All stories do. Be clear what it is, and make sure it's one that you want to send.

How Can I Tell If It Will Be Commercial?

I know that you are only in this for two basic reasons: You want to see your own words and story made into a movie—and you want to sell your script for a lot of money. If it doesn't have a good chance to sell, what's the point? So let's look at a checklist that will help us sweeten the odds.

Is it a crap shoot? Yes. Was William Goldman right when he said, "In Hollywood, nobody knows anything"? Yes. So how can you figure out if what you are about to invest many months of your life in is going to be worth it? How can you tell if it's commercial?

The "Is It Commercial?" Checklist

☑ **Do you love it?** Good. (Right answer—of course you do.) Now ask yourself, which movies you have loved in the last five years that were commercially successful? We are in a time when what is successful in movie theaters varies tremendously, from gross-out comedy to historical drama. Even quirky, arty movies are being released and making money. There is a wide spectrum of material that could be commercially successful.

Find the niche that fits you and look for some examples of movies in that niche that have been successful. If you don't remember, walk the aisles of your video store and look around.

If you can't find any precedents, but you really love it, you might want to go ahead anyway. There were no precedents for *The Blair Witch Project* or *Being John Malkovich* or *Memento* and they all worked well and did great business. Do what you love. It is a certainty that if you love it, someone else, somewhere, will get it and love it too. I am talking about love here—emotion, not intellectual stimulation. It is possible that something you find intellectually very stimulating might interest no one else. Just remember: The majority of people go to movies to feel first, and to think second. The heart has a power to connect that the mind often misses.

☑ **Is it castable?** Can you imagine well-known actors playing the leading roles? This doesn't mean every character has to be gorgeous and 30 years old. We have movie stars who are 60-ish (Harrison Ford, Al Pacino, etc.) and older (Clint Eastwood and Sean Connery). We have movie stars of all ages, from tots to tottering. But if your lead is an amoeba from the Galaxy Andromeda, a robot that looks like a garbage disposal with crab legs, a talking armadillo, or whatever least castable idea you can come up with—well, it's going to be harder to sell that script.

Don't blame Hollywood. It's our fault. Do we rush out and see the new Julia/Mel/Brad/Harrison/Tom movie the first weekend? Yes, we do. And as long as those stars open movies, Hollywood will keep buying scripts with parts for those people to play. (See more on tailoring scripts for stars in Chapter 15.)

✔ **Is it high concept?** Is it a story that can be told in a few sentences so that people understand what it's about? This doesn't mean that it has to be "Three guys make a bet they can get laid on prom night." No. It can be "Young Will Shakespeare falls in love for the first time and it helps him write Romeo and Juliet." Or: "A Roman general defies the evil emperor, is sold into slavery, and becomes a gladiator who challenges the emperor in the arena."

Spend a little time figuring out if you can tell your story in an abbreviated version. Write the ad copy. Write the *TV Guide* blurb. Write what people will tell their friends about this great movie they saw last weekend. Word of mouth is powerful—whether it comes from the guy who writes coverage on your script at the studio, from the exec who has to sell it to his boss at Universal, or from the TV spot that brings in the movie-goers.

This simple exercise, done before you begin to write the script, could be helpful all the way down the road. If you can tell it in a strong, abbreviated version now, it will be easier for you to get it right as you write. (And then to pitch it, too.)

✔ **Can you imagine the billboard?** Magazine ads? Posters? Imagine opening your newspaper to the movie section and seeing the ad for your movie. Imagine the title. The stars. The ad line. If you can visualize it, someone else can, too.

If your movie idea meets all, or nearly all, of these criteria, then you're good to go. So let's get started.

CHAPTER 2

Research

When I taught at UCLA I had two students whose methods illustrate the two extremes regarding research. One wrote a script about an Irishman who gets involved in the slave trade and piracy in the 18th century. As I read, it became obvious that he knew almost nothing about the 18th century, sailing ships, Ireland, the slave trade, Africa . . . well, let's just say it was painful.

Another student discovered a little-known landmark trial from the 1920s which involved passing a law to legalize involuntary sterilization for mentally retarded adults. He researched it deeply, but became so dedicated to the truth that he felt he couldn't write anything that he couldn't verify down to the smallest details. He was paralyzed and couldn't write the script.

These are the extreme cases—too little attention to research and too much importance placed on it. I never heard again from the student who wrote the Irish pirate story. But the other student finally broke free, incorporating the research with his own dramatic voice and vision. The script he wrote in class sold; it was produced and broadcast on network TV to critical acclaim. It launched his screenwriting career.

The moral to this story is: It is better to err on the side of thoroughness. Better to sound too smart than not smart enough.

The four primary sources of research material are paper, electronic, travel to special locations, and interviews with people.

1 Paper research: Books & periodicals. Even in the 21st century, books and articles are a central tool of writers' research. Whether you are researching a historical era, biographical material on a character or a career or technology unfamiliar to you, printed materials are an invaluable resource.

Libraries are the least expensive resource for books on all subjects. If you are not in a hurry and the books are not available in your local branch library, you can even special-order them. They will be delivered to your branch, often within a few days, courtesy of interlibrary loan service.

Used book stores can be an enormous help. Living in Portland, Oregon, I have access to Powell's Books, an independent bookstore with a huge used-book department with an inventory of over a million books. When starting a new project, I can go fill a grocery sack with books on anything from Elvis to military aircraft to forensic pathology. When I'm ready to start the next script, I just resell the stack of Elvis books back to Powell's and get store credit to fund the next research project.

2 Electronic research: The Internet. Research on the Internet gets broader and easier to access all the time. For those of you who enjoy that process, there is a world of information available. There is some danger of getting side-tracked, distracted, or overwhelmed by the amount of material available. But for certain types of information gathering, it has no rivals. I have included an appendix of websites particularly helpful to screenwriters at the back of the book.

3 Travel to special locations. Without question, this is the most fun way to research just about anything—especially if the studio is paying for it, of course.

I wrote the script for a TV movie for *The Wonderful World of Disney* on ABC called *Selma, Lord, Selma,* about the Civil Rights Movement in Alabama in 1965. I couldn't have written it if I hadn't gone to Selma and spent time talking with the people and breathing that hot, muggy air and walking those roads. The Selma in the newsreels and *Life Magazine* pictures is not the same place as the small town with Spanish moss hanging off the trees, cicadas buzzing, and people out of work, sitting on their porches, fanning themselves and watching the occasional car go by. It is a whole different place—one you can only know by going there.

Likewise, I didn't really "get" Elvis until I had walked through the tacky sadness of Graceland and stood in the tiny Sun Records studio where he made his first recordings. I needed to feel the thrill of standing in the exact spot, touching the very microphone he used.

Like Willie Nelson sings, "If you got the money, Honey, I got the time." If you have both, by all means jump on a plane. If not, try Number Four.

4 Interviews with people. The Lunch Interview is a great research tool often overlooked by writers. It can be a gold mine. If you need to know what it's like to be a P.I. or a surgeon or a deep-sea diver, take one to lunch. It is remarkable how generous people are with their expertise and how willing they are to talk about their lives if a writer offers to take them to lunch and listen.

In order to find people, you have to pick up the phone and make some calls. Call a hospital and ask for a referral for a trauma surgeon. Or call the state prison and ask if there is an organization for prisoners' wives. Start asking. You can get in touch with anyone in any field, including the C.I.A.

For the interview session, be sure to have a tape recorder handy with fresh batteries. I've done this dozens of times, and no one has ever minded being recorded. Just ask first before you turn on the machine. Notes are fine, but one of the most important aspects of this kind of research is to get the jargon of a particular field. It is essential to get the language right. You can't write *Clueless*, for example, if you don't talk to high school kids in Beverly Hills.

I once wrote an original thriller (wholly fictional) about a forensic pathologist who worked for the police and also happened to be the serial killer they were hunting. He'd murder someone, then they'd bring him the body and he'd slightly alter the evidence in his report to toy with the detective/drinking buddy trying to find him. They still rerun this movie fairly regularly, so you may have seen it. It's called *Body of Evidence* (before Madonna's movie used the same title) and starred Barry Bostwick and Margot Kidder.

To research it, I took a police forensic pathologist to lunch and interviewed him. I was bold enough to ask questions like, "What was the most interesting clue you ever found?" "What was the toughest case you ever broke?" And, "Would you mind if I used that in my script?" I incorporated the technical language he used (which I taped, of course), and the startling ideas he told me from his experience became story points in the script.

When I was writing a script that involved a rock singer who overdosed, I couldn't figure out what a doctor would say when he decided to stop trying to revive a person. "He's dead." "It's hopeless." "I give up." I couldn't think of anything that didn't sound awful. So I called up an E.R. doc and asked him what he said at that moment. What he said was, "That's it. I'm calling it. Thank you, everyone. We did everything we could." And I put that into the script word for word. It sounded real. It *was* real. And real is usually better. In a dozen drafts in development, no one ever suggested that line be changed.

Here are a few guidelines:

1 Check out the restaurant ahead of time. Make sure there is enough light to take notes and not so much noise that your tape will be unintelligible.

2 Check out your equipment. Make sure you have plenty of tape and new batteries in your recorder.

3 Have specific questions prepared. You don't just want to know, "What was it like, being a little girl in Selma, Alabama, in 1965?" You want to know, "What rhymes did you jump rope to?" "What songs did you listen to on the radio?" "What would you have bought at the dime store if you had a quarter when you were eight?" The more specific the details you gather, the richer and more authentic your writing will be.

Every detail of a screenplay doesn't have to be authentic, but it has to *sound* authentic. It has to be believable. I recently wrote a kid-driven action adventure script in which I needed to have a character tell someone how to land a 747 aircraft. I e-mailed a friend who is a retired airline pilot, and he sent me back an exact description of the process. I was able to edit it down to a quarter-page speech that sounded smart and sharp and real, because it *was* real. If I had faked this line, at least one guy in every movie theater would have flown enough to have been be able to smell the b.s.

You want the entire audience to be flying with you, completely caught up in the experience. Even the guy who *knows* how to fly.

It's worth the trouble. Besides, you never know when the exec at the studio you're trying to win over happens to be an amateur pilot. Lose him and you lose your shot.

CHAPTER 3

Three-Act Screenplay Structure

Screenplays are written in classic three-act structure. This can be summarized as: Act One, get your character up a tree. Act Two, throw rocks at him. And in Act Three, get him down. In a standard two-hour movie, you'd have roughly 30 minutes (or pages) for Act One, 60 minutes for Act Two, and another 30 minutes for Act Three. Each act has its own work to accomplish and its own difficulties. Let's walk through them, step by step.

Act One

The Set-Up. The first 15 minutes/pages are where you set up your story. Tell the audience the basic facts. Who are your main characters? Where and when does the story take place? What genre or style of movie is it? The sooner you orient your audience, the better. (If it is a comedy, it had better be funny upfront, or your audience may not get into laugh mode.) Your main character must be introduced by page 15—and generally the antagonist and love interest as well. Skilled screenwriters often use the first moments of a film to set up the theme using a symbolic image or visual message.

The Catalyst. This is the initiating event. In the first 15 minutes something happens that sets the story in motion. A problem presents itself. It could come in the form of action or dialogue. A man tells Indiana Jones that his father, while searching for the Holy Grail, has disappeared. Someone gets a letter or a phone call. Whatever form it takes, the Catalyst will pull your character into the story. It demands an action or reaction to follow. (Indy has to rush off to rescue Dad.)

The Central Question. This needs to be asked in Act One. This is a "story" question, not a thematic one. It is usually simple and is always answered by the Climax. "Will the comet destroy the earth?" "Will the boy win the girl?" "Will Indy save Dad and find the Holy Grail?" This question needs to be strongly in place by page 30.

The First Turning Point. Act One should come to a turning point between page 25 and 35. This should accomplish several things:

1. Turn the story in a new direction.
2. Set up what Act Two is going to be.
3. Raise the stakes (if possible).
4. Re-ask the Central Question—now with possibly a different outcome.

In *The Last Crusade* Indy finds Dad, but instead of rescuing him, he gets them both in hotter water and lets the Grail diary fall into the hands of the bad guys. The story turns in a new direction. Now, Indy is fleeing instead of searching. It sets up what Act Two is going to be, a father/son buddy movie. It raises the stakes: Now they're both in danger, not just Dad. And it re-asks the Central Question with possibly a different answer: Maybe the bad guys will win!

Act Two

Act Two is the main part of the story, including any thematic ideas and sub-plots. This is where you really develop your story, character, and relationships. The protagonist goes on the journey, has the adventure, takes up the challenge, flees for his life, and comes up against roadblocks and reversals. Relationships evolve. Romance blossoms. Characters develop. The going gets tough and the movie gets cooking. The plot thickens.

Act Two is the body of the film. Chapter 20 ("Act Two Blues") goes into detailed techniques for keeping this—the biggest, toughest act—working.

The Second Turning Point. This comes at the end of the second act, somewhere between pages 75 and 90. In other words, it occurs around three-quarters of the way through—page 75 if the movie is 90 minutes long, or page 90 if it's a full two hours. Like the First, the Second Turning Point needs to accomplish several things.

1. Turn the direction of the story again.
2. Raise the stakes again.
3. Start a ticking clock—if possible, launching us into Act Three and toward the Climax with heightened energy.
4. Ask the Central Question again.

In a James Bond-type movie, this is where the nuclear bomb starts counting down toward zero. It could be the darkest hour before the dawn, when things really look hopeless.

Act Three

Act Three is the race to the finish line. It should be no more than 30 pages, and it should head directly for the following:

The Climax. In action-adventure movies, this is the final conflict—whether it looks like the *Gunfight at the OK Corral*, or Luke Skywalker dive-bombing the Death Star. In a love story, it could be as simple as the two lovers finally getting together in the final clinch, or Romeo and Juliet dying. In *Casablanca*, the Climax is Rick putting Ilsa on that plane.

The Conclusion. Audiences have become accustomed to movies ending within 5 minutes after the Climax. If a movie takes longer to wrap up loose ends, they tend to lose interest. So, wrap it up quickly and FADE OUT.

Let's walk through a specific example of three-act structure. We'll use *Erin Brockovich* because it is perfectly structured and is easy to pick up at your local video/DVD rental store if you want to study it in depth.

Erin Brockovich/Act One

The Set-Up. The movie opens with the introduction of the main character—big hair, short skirts, and cleavage—on job interviews. She is humble, poorly qualified, but committed to do whatever it takes to work hard and support her kids. She strikes out, and as she gets into her old junker of a car to head home, a speeding Jaguar blows through a red light and slams into her, wrecking her car and injuring her neck. We are three minutes in and this is the Catalyst—the action that gets the story rolling. Without it this story never would have happened at all.

What happens next?

3:46 (minutes : seconds). She meets Ed Masrey, the lawyer for her personal injury case.

7:30. She loses her lawsuit and has no money, no job. She goes home to her kids. Loses her next-door babysitter. The cupboards are nearly bare and cockroaches have taken over the kitchen. So she takes the kids out to a coffee shop where they eat cheeseburgers. She lies about being hungry and only orders a cup of coffee. Later that night when her kids are safely asleep we see her eating cold food with a fork right out of the can.

Do we care about this woman? Yes. She's a good person, trying hard. She has every reason to be angry with the world or bedridden with depression, but she is neither. She's in there kicking and not complaining in front of the kids. Is she the underdog? You bet.

Two last pieces of the Set-Up are:

13:00. Thirteen minutes in, she goes to work for the lawyer, Ed Masrey. He doesn't give her a job, but she takes the initiative and makes it happen out of the sheer strength of her intention. Ed is no match for her. So now she is on her feet again—and ready to meet a guy.

And 16 minutes in, we meet the love interest, George. The biker that now lives next door with his Harley. He is interested in Erin right away. She shuts him down. A classic movie "cute meet" scene. This is the end of the Set-Up.

First Plot Point. Erin finds medical records in a real-estate file. At first this seems to be merely a mistake. Something misfiled. This is the clue, however, from which the entire mystery begins to unfold. As Erin finds more clues, this is interwoven with:

22:00. Erin loses another babysitter, and George takes over with the kids. Barbecues hot dogs for them. Plays cards with them. Makes a deal with Erin to babysit for her.

26:00. Erin finds paperwork that reveals PG&E offers to buy real estate. Also finds toxicology tests. Lymphocytes. T-cell and white-blood-cell counts. Suspicious clues.

27:30. Erin asks Ed if she can investigate the case. He says sure.

28:00. Erin drives out to Hinkley. Meets the Jensons. Finds out how sick this family is. That PG&E paid for all the medical bills. And that there was a pollution problem with some kind of chromium—which PG&E experts told the town was good for people.

First Turning Point. We are half an hour in. Can you feel the story turning? Something's coming. Suddenly the stakes have skyrocketed. This is big and it's frightening. It has just become clear to Erin (and to us) that something is very wrong in the town of Hinkley. And the main plotline begins to unfold.

This is the end of Act One. What has been accomplished with the First Turning Point?

1. The stakes are raised. The stakes have been raised from the story of the survival of one woman and her kids to many families whose lives are at risk, who have been lied to and poisoned by a powerful adversary, PG&E.

2. The whole direction shifts. The direction has changed from Erin just trying to survive to Erin on a mission: trying to solve a mystery and help others worse off than herself.

3. Sets up what Act Two is going to be about. The entire second act will be about Erin and her relationship with the town of Hinkley and its people.

4. Re-asks the central question with possibly a different likely outcome. The Central Question in this movie is "Will Erin Brockovich overcome tremendous odds (and obstacles) to become a heroine and make a difference in the world?" At the beginning of Act One this did not look at all likely, as she couldn't see past her own family's immediate survival needs. Now that has changed. She has come across a situation in which there is a small glimmer of possibility. She could make a difference here, on a bigger scale than the hand-to-mouth existence she has been living.

Erin Brockovich/Act Two

This is where the screenwriter gets to develop:

Theme. In *Erin Brockovich* the theme is: Can David beat Goliath? Can right win out over might?

Subplots. We will go into the *Erin Brockovich* subplots in detail in Chapter Five, looking at how they are woven into the main plot—how they support it and are supported in turn by it. Briefly, in Act Two the subplots are:

Subplot B. Love story between Erin and George
Subplot C. Erin's relationship with her son
Subplot D. Erin and the Water Department Guy
Subplot E. Donna Jenson

There are several others, but these are more than enough to make our points.

Through-line (the A Story). Keeping the "Through-line," also known as the "A Story," alive. That is the main, central plot, the one your protagonist is primarily engaged in.

Let's walk through Act Two of *Erin Brockovich:*
31:30. Erin goes to UCLA and asks professor about chromium. He tells

her about good and bad types. Hexavalent is the bad kind that kills people.

33:00 to 36:00. Erin goes to the County Water Board. Finds PG&E documentation of hexavalent chromium at Hinkley plant.

37:30. Erin gets fired from her job by Ed, who thought she was off having fun, not realizing she was working on the case—or even that there *is* a case. This is a *roadblock!* Remember: The more stumbling blocks you can throw into Act Two for your characters to overcome, the better. This is a good one.

39:00-42:00. Development of love story. George fixes her sink. When she cries about being fired, he comforts her. They become lovers. She has a chance to talk about her dream (theme) of making a difference in the world, remembering her idealism when she was Miss Wichita, Kansas.

42:00. Erin is back to searching want ads, with bills piling up.

43:00. Ed comes to the door with information for her from UCLA professor. Ed wants to know what that case is about. She tells him. He hires her back with a raise and benefits.

46:30. Back at Water Board. Erin gets more information and photocopies it.

48:00. Erin tells Donna Jenson that PG&E's chromium was poisonous.

50:00. PG&E sends boy attorney with $250,000 offer for the Jenson's house.

53:30. Second Hinkley family comes forward.

Halfway Point (1 hour).

1:00:00. One hour into the movie, where are we now? The real story is off and running. We go into montages of getting more and more plaintiffs in the lawsuit. The scale of the whole story has ballooned from a handful of people in the movie's first hour to hundreds in the second. Erin gathers water samples and a dead frog. Takes risks. Gets death threat on the phone. She has her son mad at her and misses her baby daughter's first word. But she is on a mission. And the ball is absolutely rolling now.

1:16:00. By this point, there are 411 plaintiffs. Ed calls it a "monster case"—expensive. They need proof that PG&E Corporate in San Francisco knew what was going on, not just the local PG&E. They need a "smoking gun."

1:18:00. Donna Jenson has new breast cancer.

1:20:00. A judge denies PG&E's attempts to get it thrown out. He says they are going to court. This is a win.

1:22:00. PG&E sends "Suits" to Masrey's office. They offer $20 million. Erin blows them out of the office and as a "button" on the scene [see page 55 for discussion of what a "button" is] tells them the water in their drinking glasses was brought in especially for them from the wells in Hinkley. Another win for our team.

1:24:00. George, neglected by her obsession with her work, breaks up with Erin and leaves them.

1:27:00. Erin now takes the kids with her to continue her work in Hinkley. The kids aren't too happy about it.

1:28:00. Erin gets toughest townsperson (Pamela) to join the lawsuit.

1:30:00. **Second Turning Point**. An hour and a half in—to the exact minute. Erin goes by the office to find that Ed has turned her case over to some bigshot lawyer played by Peter Coyote. New partners. *They'll* be handling Hinkley from now on. And Erin, of course, is furious and betrayed.

The End of Act Two

Where are we?

Erin has just lost her project, her man, her community—and even her kids don't like her much right now. Things are not looking up, which is exactly as it should be as we leave Act Two. (If things look rosy going into Act Three, you are not doing your job.)

The Second Turning Point
This should accomplish the following:

1. The direction changes. Erin's life's mission has been handed over to a complete stranger.

2. The stakes are raised. There are now over 600 plaintiffs, and their future is at risk. And the rules have changed. There will be no jury trial. And 90 percent of the plaintiffs have to sign agreements for a settlement or they won't have a case at all.

3. The clock is ticking. Court dates neatly solve this requirement.

4. The Central Question is raised again: Will Erin accomplish her mission and make a difference in the world? Not looking good now. She has been suddenly and totally disenfranchised.

Mission accomplished. Let's move on to:

Act Three

Things now have to go from bad to worse. Sure enough, the new "powerhouse" attorneys nearly ruin the case, alienating the town. People feel that Erin and Ed lied to them. They are being asked to start over from scratch, with strangers they don't know. Erin is insulted by the Suits and insults them. Tempers are running high. And they still don't have a "smoking gun" to tie PG&E Corporate to the case.

1:43:00. Town meeting. Ed convinces most of them that they need to stick together in order to win. All present sign, but Erin still needs to get another 150 signatures.

1:46:00. George reappears, but only as babysitter, not lover. Erin continues to work to get signatures.

1:52:00. **The Third Act Turning Point.** In a bar, a creepy guy comes on to Erin—and turns out to be the guy with the smoking gun they need to nail PG&E. He has documentation that PG&E Corporate knew. This is the final piece they need to win the day.

The Climax

1:57:00. This is Erin's big scene: showing up the Suits by walking in with the smoking gun and all 634 signatures. She has accomplished a seemingly impossible task. When they ask her how, she says that, since she has no brains and no skills, she had to perform 634 sexual favors. The "button" on the scene is, "I'm really quite tired."

The Conclusion

2:00:00. George and Erin drive out together so she can share with him the reward for which both of them and the kids gave up so much. They go to the Jensons' and tell Donna that she has been awarded $5 million. This answers the plot question of "Will David beat Goliath?" And it also answers the B Story question, "Will Erin and George work it out?" For movie purposes, yes. Here they are together for the most important moment in Erin's life.

The Tag and the Button

This wraps it all up. Masrey has gorgeous new law offices, and Erin's office is a beauty. Ed comes in and gives her her bonus: $2 million. Did this under-dog beat the odds and make a difference in the world? Absolutely. It's a complete win.

From Climax to FADE OUT: 4 minutes. Finish the story and wrap it up.

There you have it: the Three-Act Structure, seen in the movie *Erin Brockovich*. Get your hero up a tree, throw rocks at her, and get her down again. It's not so complicated, is it?

Easy as one, two, three.

CHAPTER 4

Scene Cards and the Storyboard

One of the most useful things screenwriters learn at film school is how to use scene cards to create a storyboard before they begin writing a script. In case you skipped film school (or plan to), here are the basics of that class.

Making Scene Cards

What are Scene Cards? As their name implies, these are only for scenes, one card per scene. Don't add background character descriptions, details, or dialogue. Just lay out the scene as briefly as possible. Example: A single card from *Romeo and Juliet* might read:

> Plaza. Verona. Day.
> Fight between Tybalt and Mercutio.
> Romeo tries to stop it.
> T. kills M. R. kills T.

I recommend that you use standard 3″ x 5″ file cards. Post-its will stick together and make you crazy. And larger cards take too much space to lay out. On 3 x 5 cards, a feature-length script can be laid out on your dining-room table or even on a good-sized coffee table.

Start with a pile. I always begin by making four "free" cards. The working title goes on one, and the phrases Act One, Act Two, and Act Three go on the three others. That way, I already have a pile started before coming up with a single scene. Don't begin laying the cards out until you get a good-sized pile, at least 30 to 40 cards.

The Obligatory Scenes. Start with the scenes you know you have to have, without which you couldn't tell the story. Your premise will demand them. Example: In a love story, Boy has to meet Girl. In a thriller, you must introduce the Bad Guy. You know the scenes I mean.

Things you'd love to see in this movie. You've put in the required basic-story scenes, now throw in those imaginative, fun things. Probably not all of these will end up in the script, but this is the time to let your imagination go wide and wild. Maybe one of the scenes could take place in a hot-air balloon. Maybe a tornado blows through. Anything can happen. Film is a visual medium. Let yourself get visually creative.

Subplots. We'll go into detail in the next chapter on what subplots are and how to structure them, but for now, if you know some subplots you want to use, make the cards for them. I put a different-colored dot on the corner of appropriate scene cards to indicate each subplot. That way, I can glance over the storyboard and see visually that I have woven a subplot into the main story line smoothly. I might use a pink dot for the love-story subplot. Or a blue dot for an ongoing running-joke subplot involving a dog. Or a red dot for the villain, to be sure he doesn't disappear for too many scenes in a row. The abstract theory of interweaving your story threads takes on a more immediate reality once you begin to visually track the colored dots scattered across your storyboard.

Laying Out the Cards

How many cards should you have? By the end of this process you will have a whole movie's worth, but for right now, write the ones you know, and then go ahead and begin laying out the storyboard.

By the time you have finished this process, you should have around 50 cards, though anything from 40 to 65 can work. Scenes average about 2 pages each. Some will be only ⅛ page and others 5 pages, but they should average out to around 60 cards for a 120-page script (which equals a two-hour movie).

Start laying out the cards from the beginning. Once you have a good-sized pile of cards, it is time to start laying them out on a tabletop in a "storyboard," in columns starting with the title and Act One in the upper left and working down one column, then starting at the top again. Usually, you start out with a good sense of how the story begins. You will probably be able to lay out the Set-Up and much of Act One fairly easily.

Then you'll get to a point, possibly early in Act Two, where you aren't sure what happens next.

Strategies for Laying Out the Cards

Skip to the end. You may not know the middle, but you usually know how the story ends. Boy gets Girl. Bad Guy gets his due. Start from the end and work your way backwards, from the denouement to the climax—and on toward the middle, until you don't know what happens next.

Lay out both ends of the bridge. As you lay out the cards on a tabletop, first lay out the beginning as far as it goes. Then lay out the end and work your way backwards. What you now have is a bridge with a gap in the middle of the second act, or possibly even a huge gap where the second act should be. Don't panic.

Start filling in the gap. What scenes can you come up with to fill in that empty space? What could happen? Find ways to make it harder for your protagonist. Throw stumbling blocks and reversals into his/her path. Complicate things.

Make sure each domino hits another domino. If you have a scene card that isn't triggered by a preceding scene or doesn't trigger the next, this could be a problem. You may have one card you keep moving around that doesn't fit in anywhere. Set it aside. Later, you may be able to combine it with another scene and make it fit perfectly. You may end up with a whole pile of "Maybe's." That's fine. Just set it to one side. Ideally every scene should trigger the next—like a perfectly placed row of dominoes. Keeping this concept in mind will also make the writing process much easier when you get to that stage.

Place the Act Cards where they belong. Acts One and Three should be about equal in length, with Act Two being about twice as long. In other words, when laid out on a table, Act One should be one column, Act Two two columns, and Act Three one column—all the columns being of roughly equal lengths.

If this is how your cards look, congratulations! You already have a well-balanced, structured script. If not, tinker. Find ways to tighten a first act. Or complicate, expand, or throw some unexpected twists or surprises into the second or third acts.

It may seem glamorous to invest in a large bulletin board and pin your scene cards to it. A lot of screenwriters do this. Personally, I prefer to lay the cards out on a table. For one thing, on a bulletin board, if I want to change just three scenes, I'd have to untack all of them and move them all. Whereas it takes just moments to slide the cards around into new spots on a table.

Also, sometimes cards pinned to the wall begin to blend into the wall-paper. As I lay out the cards newly at the beginning of each workday, I keep seeing them with a fresh eye.

A bulletin board definitely looks cool. But beware: As friends drop by, they will read the cards and want you to explain the scenes and the process to them. Or worse, they will offer "helpful" criticism. This stage of the process should be held *sacred*. As in *secret*. As in *"butt out."*

Pick them up and lay them down. Next, gather all the cards into a single pile, in order, with the first card on top. Now, lay them out again—while telling yourself the story out loud.

This is an excellent way to find the holes. As you tell the story to your-self, you will find a place that doesn't flow right. You'll notice one scene that doesn't seem to lead to the next (or anywhere near it). Stop and work that spot—rearrange a couple of scenes, or add something, or drop something.

There is a right way to tell each story. (And as many right ways as there are stories.) Just keep working with the cards until they feel right for *this* story.

Write your script from the stacked deck. Once the cards are working well, I set the stack on my mousepad. I'll write a scene, then flip that card over and proceed to the next. It's like having a well-planned cheat sheet. Still, know that there will come a point when the next scene in the pile doesn't work. After all, your structurally smart Left Brain planned this thing. And your creatively wonderful Right Brain is now writing the script. That's okay. When that happens, I usually flip a few cards over until I get to a scene that does feel right.

Usually, halfway through writing the script, I need to stop and lay out the last 30 cards again, restructuring them somewhat—now knowing how it's all going to play out.

I keep all of my sets of scene cards in cardboard 3 x 5 file boxes, alphabetically by title. It occasionally happens that you need to write another draft later (sometimes years later), and it speeds things up if you can pull the deck of cards magically from your sleeve and reshuffle.

A Sample Storyboard

Let's walk through one. How about "Cinderella, Set in Beverly Hills High School Class of 2003"? Let's call her Courtney.

1 Get a pack of 3 x 5 cards.

2 Write out your "free cards."
Write down the working title (Cinderella/BHHS '03) and the "header" cards for Acts One, Two, and Three.

3 Write down the Obligatory Scenes.
Courtney meets the football hero/prince.
The ball/prom scene. (Gotta have it!)
She magically gets a dress.
Introduce her lousy homelife, mean stepmother.
Maybe her wicked stepsisters, Brittany and Tiffany, go to her school. Introduce them.

Show a scene where they are mean to her or embarrass her at school. She gets invited to the prom.

Get the idea? There are always quite a few scenes without which you can't tell the story.

4 **Throw in some Fun Stuff**. What would be great to see in this movie?
The wicked stepsisters getting trashed at the prom?
Falling into the hotel pool maybe?
Maybe there's a local parade in which the homecoming princesses ride on a float and Brittany and Tiffany get paid back in mid-parade.
Maybe Courtney has a demeaning fast-food job instead of working at home in the kitchen like Cinderella did.
The fairy godmother could be a bag lady—with a 1930s ballgown stashed away.
The chariot could be a limo moonlighting between another job's drop-off and pickup, which is why he has to leave at midnight on the dot.
And on and on.

5 **Lay out the cards**.
Act One sets up Courtney's situation, introduces her to the prince, and sets up the upcoming prom (to which Courtney's not invited).
Act Two: Courtney finds a way to get to the prom while WSM and B & T try to undermine her. Fairy godmother needed to be introduced back in Act One, but she gets more involved in Act Two. And Courtney falls more in love with the prince. Act Two climaxes with the prom—of course.
Act Three is the search for that fabulous girl.

See? It's not hard. Take it one scene at a time. Lay those cards out and get them working before you write FADE IN. Too many screenwriters begin writing without structuring scene cards and a storyboard. And they soon find themselves mind-boggled and bogged down . . . and never make it to the final FADE OUT.

CHAPTER 5

Subplots: Weaving Together A, B & C Stories

The subplots, of course, are the other story threads that interweave throughout the screenplay to make it rich, colorful, and compelling. Nearly all screenplays have subplots. Some have a dozen of them. We'll look at the subplots in *Erin Brockovich* to learn how to create them, weave them into a script, and use them to help create a great movie. First, there are a few rules to cover.

1 **Each subplot needs to intrinsically connect to and support the Main Plot**. Subplots need to support and promote the Main Plot (also called the A Story or the Through-line). And if the main story also supports the subplot in turn, it's even stronger. Erin's mission (A Story) fuels the problems she's having with her kid. And having problems with her kid (B Story) raises the stakes on her mission itself.

If a subplot can be cut and the main story is not impacted at all, cut it. It will end up on the cutting-room floor later anyway. Save the money. Lose it now.

Is it your favorite thing and you can't bear to lose it? Then find a way to hook it into your A Story. You can do it. Get creative.

2 **Each subplot needs to be structured with at least three beats**. A subplot needs a beginning, a middle, and an end. It needs at least three beats, or scenes.

3 **Each subplot needs to be thematically aligned with the whole**. In other words, you don't have an A Story that says "The underdog can win"—and a B Story that says "Life is pointless."

4 Each subplot needs to match the A Story in style and tone. A subplot must easily exist in the same reality. You can't have a gritty, reality-based A Story and a *Looney Tunes* B Story.

Enough about rules. Let's shuffle the cards and deal out a few hands to see how the game is played. In *Erin Brockovich*, the Love Story might be called the B Story. Let's look at that subplot first.

B Story / George and Erin

B Story: Act One

16 minutes in. Erin meets handsome George, the biker next door.

22-25 min. George rescues kids from babysitter who dumped them. He barbecues hotdogs for them, plays cards with them. Offers to be the new babysitter, and Erin says okay.

38 min. George fixes the sink. She tells him she got fired. She cries. He comforts her.

39-42 min. **B Story's Act One Turning Point.** They become lovers. She tells him her idealistic dreams and about being Miss Wichita. Bed-play with tiara.

For the Love Story (B Story), the "Act One" Turning Point is: Girl gets guy. Note: This Turning Point for the "Act One" of the B Story does not occur in the Act One of the A Story, but in the movie's Act Two. In other words, each subplot has its own structure and its own timing of its act breaks.

B Story: Act Two

55:30. Erin comes home to G. and kids. G. tells her her son is mad at her for not being around.

1:07:00. George plays Monopoly with the kids. Erin gets a threatening phone call. G. is protective. Erin is rude to him.

1:10:00. Late-night call to George while driving. He tells her about her baby's first word, "ball." She cries. Intimate moment. He's with kids. She's missing it.

1:14:30. At picnic. George treated like babysitter. Sees Harleys blow by. He's stuck taking care of kids. She sends him home with kids while she stays on alone.

1:24:00. **B Story's Act Two Turning Point.** George has had enough. He bought her a present to give her the next time she was nice to him, but she hasn't been nice to him in months. She got a raise. She can afford to hire a babysitter, so she doesn't need him any more. He leaves her.

This is the Act Two Turning Point of the B Story: Girl loses guy.

B Story: Act Three

1:32:00. Erin sees George ride off on his motorcycle. He doesn't even look back.

1:46:00. George reappears at a motel in Hinkley to watch the kids while she works for a few days. They are not back together. He's only there for the kids. But she tells him she is sorry.

1:49:00. George takes the kids out to breakfast. Erin still in bed.

1:59:00. **B Story's Climax and Conclusion.** George drives out to Hinkley with Erin to share the big moment. Donna Jenson getting $5 million settlement. The two of them share the joy of the victory.

Laid out like this, it should be easy to see how the B Story subplot is carefully structured. It has a beginning, middle, and end. It has its own three-act structure.

Act One: They meet, fall in love, share a family. The First Turning Point is when they become lovers.

Act Two: He takes care of the kids while she neglects them all, obsessed with her mission. He is neglected, hurt, leaves. This is the Second Turning Point.

Act Three: He is a good man and still comes through for her again. She's sorry. They get back together.

The Climax of the B Story is also the Climax of the A Story. It's pretty simple. This subplot also completely supports the A Story, which is Erin's heroic journey. Erin has to succeed in her big mission while caring for her kids. Without George's love and help, she might not have been able to do this. The George scenes are the main ones in which we see what the mission costs Erin personally. Without them, the movie would have lost a big piece of its humanity. It would be missing its heart.

You have also noticed that the B Story's acts do not necessarily fall into the same three-act divisions as the A Story. In fact, some of the additional subplots listed below are not even introduced until Act Two of the main storyline. This is not only natural, it's a good thing. Every time any of the plots or subplots has a turning point, it creates a surge of energy. Things turn in a new direction, creating new possibilities and generating new interest. Having subplots with turning points in the middle of the second act, for instance, can really help liven the story up and keep it exciting or emotionally compelling.

Let's play another round. Some of the subplots are so simple that they only have three beats or so. Let's look at some of the minor stories for *Erin Brockovich* that come further down the list.

C Story / Charles Embry

In the movie, this role is played by Tracey Walter. This subplot doesn't begin until late in Act Two of the movie. At first, it feels like a threat. Not until its third act does Erin realize it is actually the godsend they have needed. This subplot offers the answer to their biggest problem: how to tie PG&E Corporate to the whole drama in Hinkley.

1:12:00. **Beat One.** Picnic in Hinkley. She sees Embry and he sees her. They exchange a few words.

1:43:00. **Beat Two.** Town Hall Meeting. Embry is there. He smiles at Erin.

1:52:00. **Beat Three.** Late night at a bar. At first Embry seems like a threat, possibly even dangerous. Then, he's more like a strange lonely guy trying to pick her up. But after a few minutes, she realizes that he is there to help. He's from inside PG&E. And he actually has the "smoking gun" and gives it to her: a letter from Corporate admitting their knowledge of the whole thing. It is the ace that wins the game.

This entire subplot only has three scenes. But it can have no less. If we had never seen Embry until the bar scene, it would have been *deus ex machina*—the answer dropped out of a clear blue sky (not sound story-telling). The earlier beats gave him a reality in the story and led us to the major turning-point of the story that he becomes. Three beats is the minimum. Don't try to shortcut this rule.

D Story / Erin's Son

We've seen him many times as one of Erin's kids. But as a character in conflict with the main character he has three basic beats.

55:30. **Beat One.** When Erin comes home late, George tells her that her son is mad at her. She goes into the bedroom to talk to him and he is very angry with her. She tries to talk to him, but can't get through to him.

1:29:30. **Beat Two.** After George has left, Erin is dragging the kids around with her. Her son is really mad at her, but no more silent treatment. He is yelling at her as they walk across the parking lot to work. Telling her she's not as good a mother as his friends' moms.

1:49:00. **Beat Three.** At a motel, when George is taking the kids to breakfast and Erin is lying on the couch, her son has read the papers on one of the children from Hinkley and asks her about it. When she explains about the sick little girl who is just his age, he understands what his mom's work is about and offers to bring her back some scrambled eggs. It's a simple moment that translates into forgiveness, understanding, and love. It's the healing of a relationship and the resolution of a subplot.

Three beats. Simple. But as before, this subplot ties directly into the main storyline. It supports the A Story, just as the A Story supports it in return. It is like architecture. All the walls and beams need to work together to hold up the roof. The subplots are those walls and beams. They are load-bearing and necessary.

And if they turn out to be just garden sheds, raze them!

To switch metaphors, keep only those threads whose weaving is interconnected and interdependent to the whole fabric.

If you'd like to try a few more on your own, try tracking these other *Erin Brockovich* subplots:

Pamela (the reluctant plaintiff played by Cherry Jones)
The Water Board Guy
Babysitter Saga
Trail of the Smoking Gun
Tracking Chromium
Parents with Dying Daughter

Each subplot has at least three beats. Each supports the A Story and is nearly inextricably tied to it. The writer, Susannah Grant, did a beautiful job in crafting this script and richly deserves all the accolades and rewards her good work has earned.

When I am laying out my subplots in the Scene Card/Storyboard phase of the process, as I mentioned earlier, I will put a colored dot in the corner of all the cards from one subplot. For example, I would have put a pink dot in the corner of every card for the love-story subplot. And a green dot for every scene with Erin's kids. Then I can stand back and look at the cards spread out on the table and tell easily which storylines I have abandoned for too long—and which may be in danger of beginning to dominate the A Story.

When my cards have colors evenly woven through, with balance and continuity, like a good tapestry, I know I'm getting it right. Once this work is done, I am ready to begin writing a screenplay.

Begin to look closely at other movies and notice how the subplots work (or don't work). Not all movies are as well crafted as *Erin Brockovich*. But there are lessons to be learned from them all.

CHAPTER 6

The Levels of Character Evolution

I**t's one thing to have a story come full circle,** but you don't want your protagonist to come back to where he/she began as a character. It is essential that he or she grows, changes, learns something in the course of the movie. In screenwriting this is called the "Character Arc." To have a character learn nothing leaves the audience with a "so what?" feeling. Why have we bothered going on this journey if nothing was learned from it?

Teaching Screenwriting at UCLA Film School a few years ago, I developed a structure for understanding character evolution, breaking it down into five levels. Once we lay them out, we'll go into examples of how characters move through them. These levels can be thought of as the character's perspective, beginning with the lowest level of focusing only on himself, then his focus begins moving upward and outward, hopefully all the way to the far horizon.

Character Evolution

Level One: Self. A Level One character is still at survival level, completely self-centered. This character's value system is simple: I, me, mine. He is the proverbial Lone Wolf, looking out for Number One. He is selfish, self-serving and often self-obsessed. This does not make for a very sympathetic character, but in movies, Level One protagonists almost always move up to a higher level before the end.

Level Two: Bonding. Here, the character's perspective encompasses two people. Often these are lovers, but they could also be partners, siblings, or parent and child. The viewpoint of the Level Two character is: The two of us are all that matters. "I got my girl, who could ask for anything more?" Think police partners. Butch and Sundance. Bonnie and Clyde. Romeo and Juliet. A mother bear with a cub. Level Two pairs are self-contained and exclusive. If they are lovers, it is the kind of relationship where they could lock themselves in a motel room for a week and, short of nuclear war, not give a damn about anything in the outside world.

Level Three: Family. A Level Three character is centered in Clan mentality. "Godfather" mentality—a person enmeshed in and loyal to a group of any size that excludes others. He or she thinks: Me and mine. Forget the rest of the world; my family is all that matters. The "family" could be any small, closed group. An army platoon, football team, group of prisoners, street gang, or actual family that is threatened will build this kind of wall around itself.

A Level Three character is anyone completely immersed within that group's structure. Think of the platoon sergeant in any war movie you can name, or Michael Corleone in *The Godfather*. Their points of view do not extend beyond those familial ties.

Level Four: Community. As the character raises his focus, he/she begins to see the whole community and begins to think more in terms of the good of the larger group. This character thinks: My community, my country. The horizon widens to include a broader arena. War heroes showered with medals and the highest honors (even though they may have slaughtered innocents of the enemy nation) are the epitome of Level Four thinking. A Level Four character may have risked life and limb for the greater good, but not the good of all. That would be the next level.

Level Five: Humanity. This is the level at which people like Gandhi, Martin Luther King, Jr., and Mother Theresa lived. A Level Five character lives in a more spiritually enlightened reality, recognizing the value of every human being. Level Five often involves the character's relationship to God or an awareness of moral responsibility to the planet. Think: selfless. Spiritual epiphany. Filled with love and joy.

How it Works

Now for the fun part. How do these levels actually work? And why are these levels of character evolution important to a screenwriter?

In movie terms, any time you move a character from one level up to another, you create a surge of energy, inspiration, or aliveness in your audience. People love to participate in these shifts in character evolution—even if the character only moves up one level.

In *Rainman*, for instance, Tom Cruise's character is a typical Level One guy. He's completely self-involved, a jerk to his girlfriend, and ruthless in business. No family, no friends; he's alone in the world. His only interest is looking out for Number One. When he finds out he has an autistic brother, played by Dustin Hoffman, his only thought is how to exploit him to meet his own selfish, monetary needs. Then gradually, in spite of all his resistance, they bond. By the end he has made his brother's well-being his priority and has come to love him. And it gets us. He has only shifted from Level One to Level Two, and we're moved.

In *Casablanca*, Rick (Bogart) is a classic Level One. He had been at Level Two in the past, falling in love, but it didn't work out, so he reverted to Level One. When his old love walks into his nightclub, he recovers to Level Two, but doesn't stop there. By the end, he is standing firmly on Level Four, sacrificing his personal desires for the good of the cause (i.e., the community). This is a Level One to Level Four evolution and we love it. As a result, *Casablanca* is a classic favorite that we watch again and again.

It's not by chance that *Funny Girl* starts with "I'm The Greatest Star" and ends with "Oh, my man I love him so . . ." Or that *How To Succeed In Business Without Really Trying* opens with the title song and builds to "The Brotherhood of Man." Fanny Brice and J. Pierpont Finch were both Level Ones—and both moved up.

Character Levels and Relationships

If two people are at developmental levels that are too far apart, it's unlikely that any real connection can take place between them. It's unbelievable they could have a good, healthy relationship. Going back to *Casablanca*, for instance, Ilsa almost abandons the cause because of her love for Rick, but she is a true Level Four character, and this would have been a tragic loss of character development for her. In order to keep her from coming down to his level, Rick has to come up to hers, to Level Four. She can love her man, but she can't live in his world and still be true to herself and her ideals. So he has to move up or lose her.

Complete Transformation: Level One to Level Five

They are rare, but I have found two examples of complete Level One to Five evolution, and both movies are so popular as to be overdone (and over-shown) yearly.

Dickens' *A Christmas Carol* has the most definitive Level One character in the miserly Ebenezer Scrooge. Guided by three ghosts, he climbs up all five levels in perfect evolutionary order. The Ghost of Christmas Past shows him his childhood bond with his sister and, in young adulthood, his first love, poignantly reminding Scrooge of his own Level Two (Bonding) potential.

The Ghost of Christmas Present takes Scrooge to the Cratchits' home and to the home of his nephew's family, which Scrooge has shunned, demonstrating the joys of Family (Level 3).

The Ghost of Christmas Future shows the old miser his own Community celebrating his death because he failed them so thoroughly in life (Level Four). Finally, Scrooge sees a vision of his own eternal damnation for having so completely failed to make a contribution to Humanity while alive (Level Five). When he awakes at the end and finds it is still Christmas morning, he leaps out into the world in a state of ecstasy, bursting with love and joy for everyone on earth. That is a complete transformation. Level One to Level Five. Scrooge is a new man. And we are thrilled to leap out into that snowy street with him, in touch once again with the true spirit of Christmas.

We make a new movie version of *A Christmas Carol* every decade and rerun them on television yearly. Live theaters all over the world perform the play every December. That is the power of full character evolution: Transformation.

Another five-level evolution is one of America's favorite films: Frank Capra's *It's A Wonderful Life*. George Bailey (Jimmy Stewart) starts out just wanting to get out of his small town and explore the world. He has a passionate dream to be an adventurous explorer and has even bought the suitcase. Now, we don't really believe that George is a true Level One because, well . . . because he's Jimmy Stewart. But this is a story we want to be told, so we gladly accept it.

George's plans for adventure are abandoned when he falls in love with Mary (Donna Reed), pulling him up to Level Two. They have "a bunch of kids" (Level Three). George helps his community (via the Building and Loan Co.), risking his family's security to help his town stay afloat during the Depression (Level Four). Finally, in a crisis, he has to confront his own existence, look death in the face, and discover his purpose in life. Through that near-death experience, George Bailey emerges transformed into a Level Five man.

When he gets his life back, like Ebenezer, George Bailey is in a transformed state, filled with great joy and love for all people, even his bitterest enemy, Mr. Potter (Lionel Barrymore). We can't get enough of it. We watch it over and over—and cry every time he finds Zuzu's petals in his pocket.

Devolution of Character = Tragedy

Conversely, if you take a character down through any number of levels, it becomes tragedy, the devolution of character. In *The Godfather* trilogy, Michael Corleone (Pacino) starts out as a good Level Four guy, still in uniform from serving his country. From there, he is pulled back into the Family (Level Three). And he continues to devolve, losing his family, one by one, until finally, by the end of Part 3, he dies completely alone (Level One). This is a tragedy: His life is destroyed by the choices he has made.

Similarly, *King Lear* starts out with the king focused on his kingdom (Four), then begins devolving as he divides the kingdom among his family (Three). His world shrinks until it is just himself and his daughter Cordelia (Two). Finally, he too is alone (One), bereft, destroyed, a decrepit madman wandering the moor, howling into the wind. Once a character starts on the path of devolution, it can be a devastating and rapid downhill slide.

Level Zero: Animal Mentality

This is not a moral judgment, but indicates a very low level of mental processing. It is human being as animal—as in a young *Tarzan*, or Truffaut's *Wild Child*. Jodie Foster in *Nell* is another example. *Quest for Fire* is a classic Level Zero story of the evolution of man from a primitive ape creature to a human man standing upright, able to create fire.

Level Zero as comedy might be *Encino Man*.

The shift from Level Zero (acting or thinking like a wild animal), evolving up even a single step to a Level One, can be deeply moving. For example, the pump scene at the end of *The Miracle Worker*, when the child Helen Keller is able to communicate and understand for the first time is one of the great transformation scenes in movies and theater.

Sub-Zero Levels: Human Being as Inhuman Monster

This level of character is rarely the protagonist, and rarely ever makes any shift of consciousness. These are your sociopaths, psychopaths, sadists, Gestapo, and serial murderer types. Hannibal Lecter is the only one in this category that comes to mind as a recent Sub-zero Level protagonist. Count Dracula was a member of this group. Not much can be said in terms of evolution here, but we need to include this as a category of character. They exist.

Why Is It Important to Have Characters Evolve?

I was speaking about this to a group recently, and one of them, a doctor, came up to me afterwards and told me that when an electron changes orbits, energy is released. Isn't it marvelous when a law of physics reflects what we have discovered for ourselves in art? When a character believably shifts to a higher level of consciousness, energy is released. A surge of emotion is generated in the audience. This is the very magic we are seeking. When this magic happens—when you create it and the audience gets it—the viewers walk out of the theater, not just satisfied but uplifted as well. And isn't that what we came for?

Applying the Theory of Evolution to Your Script

How do you apply this information to the main characters in your own screenplays? Ask yourself these questions about your protagonist.

☑ **What level is she on at the beginning?**

☑ **What is important to her?**

☑ **What does she want? What are her goals?**

☑ **What changes her?**

☑ **What level is she on at the final FADE OUT?**

☑ **How do I show this transformation as an act or action?** You want to have your character show it, rather than telling the audience, "I'm a better person."

Rocky yells "Adrian!" Rick puts Ilsa on the plane. And old Ebenezer Scrooge becomes Father Christmas himself, lavishing gifts on one and all. Screenwriters are gods, especially in writing any first draft or on spec. Be conscious of the evolutionary process as you guide these mortals' lives.

CHAPTER 7

Conflict

A **few years ago I picked up a little book** called *The Christmas Box*. It was a real phenomenon, a huge bestseller. By page 10, I was bored. By page 50, I hated this book. I was angry. I wanted to call up somebody and vent my irritation over this stupid book. Why? It was a lovely book about a nice family who go to live in a gorgeous mansion with a nice old lady. So what's the problem? That's it exactly. There *was* no problem. *And if you don't have a problem, you don't have a story*.

Until a problem appears, the story hasn't started. Everything that comes before is just setup, background, exposition. Unfortunately, *The Christmas Box* never did turn out to have a story. When I saw that it had been developed for a television movie, my first thought was, "I'll bet they made the old lady not so nice." It was the most obvious option for trying to get a problem into this unbearably sweet confection. Sure enough, I turned it on, and this nice family goes to live with an unpleasant old lady with problems from the past. It wasn't enough of a problem to make a great movie, but at least it was a problem.

I admit I have made my own Christmas Box mistake. Mine was called *Grace Kelly*, a TV movie starring Cheryl Ladd. When they called and offered it to me, I was thrilled. I thought, "Fifties, Hollywood, Oscars, Prince Charming—Great!" What I should have asked is, "What's the problem?" Gorgeous rich girl goes to New York, becomes an actress, is snapped up by Hollywood, becomes a movie star, wins an Oscar, falls in love and marries a prince. Right? No problem. No story. It turned into a rather classy-looking parade of good wigs and costumes, but was an embarrassment to me as a writer. I learned the hard way by making the mistake. You be smarter. Ask the question first.

A lot of us, when we first start writing screenplays, tend to be fond of our characters, so we don't want anything too terrible to happen to them. We make it too easy for them to solve everything that comes along. We tend to wrap things up neatly at the end of each scene. We mean well, but we make it much harder for the story to work.

Conflict is the heart of the story in a very real sense. It is what keeps it pumping, makes the blood race through its veins, and brings it to *life*. In a screenplay you have to have it in every single scene. If you don't have conflict, you'd better create it.

Once you've got the problem in play, how can you strengthen it? What can you do to beef it up? The stronger the conflict, the more energy is generated in your screenplay. Ideally you want your opposing forces to be like two powerful freight trains on the same track headed toward each other on a collision course.

Here is my favorite example of a great movie train wreck by two powerful and worthy opponents, Randall McMurphy (Jack Nicholson) and Big Nurse Ratched (Louise Fletcher) in *One Flew Over the Cuckoo's Nest*. This is pure magic conjured out of thin air by the writer.

The problem: Mac wants to watch the World Series on TV and Big Nurse says no. Not much at stake? You'd think not, but you'd be wrong. Let's walk through it and see how it plays out.

Setting: A mental hospital around 1970. Mac is there as a transfer from a prison sentence. He faked mental illness, figuring it'd be easier to break out of a state sanitarium. First McMurphy brings up the idea of watching the game on TV in the daily group therapy session. Nurse Ratched says, fine, let's take a vote. McMurphy raises his hand but the other eight guys are afraid to stand up to her. He loses eight to one.

That night Mac is angry, sulks, won't play cards, doesn't like them any more. The next day, one of the other guys, Chez, brings it up again. There's another World Series game today. Fine, let's vote again. The two of them raise their hands and slowly the others follow. They win, nine to zero. It's unanimous. A landslide victory. But Nurse Ratched calmly says, "No. There are eighteen men on this ward and you need a majority." She is referring to the "vegetables" in beds and wheelchairs scattered around. McMurphy gets furious. You're not going to count *them?* But Nurse Ratched says they are human beings and they have rights as well—and the rule is you have to have a majority.

So he runs around the ward trying to enlist at least one of these guys in beds and wheelchairs. They really are catatonic or unreachable schizophrenics, totally disconnected from the real world. Finally, Big Chief pushing his broom stops and looks at McMurphy and slowly raises his hand. McMurphy whoops in victory back to the group. The Chief raised his hand! We have a majority! Ten to eight!

But no. She quietly explains that the meeting was adjourned while he was running around and the vote was closed. Period. He starts screaming, you're not going to pull that *now!* But she is unimpressed and goes quietly into the nurses' station and slides the glass window closed.

The victory has spun around into total defeat with no recourse. The other guys, depressed, slowly shuffle off to the showers while McMurphy seethes, raging, looking for any possible way to beat this monster female that has him by the short ones.

He looks up at the dead gray TV bolted to the ceiling. He doesn't even have the power to push that little button. Screw it! He looks at that screen and begins calling the plays of the World Series game as if he were the announcer. The other guys hear him and peek out to see if it's the game. No, the TV is dark. But McMurphy goes on calling the game, building the excitement as the Red Sox get a man on base. The other guys come back and start cheering their team and soon they are all watching the dark TV and the imaginary World Series, not quite sure if they're crazy or if Mac is, but they're having a damn great time and they are watching the goddam World frigging Series.

Victory! McMurphy beats her. She looks out from behind the cold glass with vicious hatred. And we love it because he beat her and she knows it. It is thrilling.

How can it be so packed with energy? Rent this movie. It crackles with electricity. And what are the stakes? Watching TV? How low can stakes be?

What is really on the line here, of course, is not a TV program. These guys' manhood is at stake here. She's not just taking away their freedom, she's busting their balls.

What makes this work? What is the engine that drives this scene? Good writing? Great acting? No. This whole deal is fueled by the power of the opposing force. By the force of Nurse Ratched's "No." And even though it is voiced in the most chilling of soft, gentle tones, it is carved in granite. Its roots go all the way to the center of the earth.

The lesson: If you want to beef up the conflict, beef up the opposing force.

In other words, if you want things to really smoke, in Act One get your character up a really *tall* tree, get him out there on skinny, cracking branches—and throw bigger and sharper rocks, hard and fast. When the going gets really tough for your characters, now you're cookin'!

CHAPTER 8

The Ticking Clock

In screenwriting, one of the hardest things to do well is the passage of time. The more time involved in the story, the harder it is to have a script that flows smoothly. Here are a few tricks of the time trade.

1 Are we there yet? It is essential that an audience has some clue as to how much time is going to transpire during the story. They don't have to know it consciously, but they have to have some sense of it. If *The Lion King* opens with the birth of the cub, Simba, subconsciously we are not at all surprised to have it end with the birth of Simba's cub; we have have come full circle. (The song is even called "The Circle of Life.")

The movie *The World According to Garp* begins with Garp's birth. Whether we know it consciously or unconsciously, we have a sense that it will end with his death, which it does.

2 Shorter is better. A few years ago a bestselling novel *Six Days of the Condor* became a hit movie starring Robert Redford, titled, you guessed it: *Three Days of the Condor*. Why? Because it's a lot easier to make an exciting three days than to hold the suspense for six. Shorter yet was the movie, *48 Hours,* in which a cop springs a criminal out of prison for the weekend to help him catch a really bad guy. Almost any of us could have made this work. Eddie Murphy and Nick Nolte chasing bad guys for two days? Piece of cake.

American Graffiti started at sunset and ended at dawn the next morning. But the world's record for shortest time span of a story in a feature film has to be *Run, Lola, Run*. The movie lasts 90 minutes, the story takes place in 20. Check it out at your video store.

The lesson: Cram your movie into the shortest workable time frame it will fit into.

3 Go long and lose 'em. I was about half an hour into watching *Bicentennial Man* (starring Robin Williams as a robot), when I realized with a shudder that, "Oh my God . . . it's called *Bicentennial Man* because the story lasts 200 years!" And it does. The audience has to watch all of the human characters get old and die, and their grandchildren get old and die. My own feeling was, "Get me out of this theater!" It is nearly impossible to make this concept work, and it worked miserably here.

In Spielberg's *A.I.* (Artificial Intelligence), the story lasts 2,000 years. Even the popmaster himself couldn't make that work.

If you engage the audience with a strong enough story, they will go almost anywhere with you, but don't stretch the time frame beyond an audience's capacity. It'll snap—and you'll lose them.

4 As time goes by. If you are committed to a story that has to cover decades, such as a biography, obviously you can't show everything. Once you have selected the events you want, how do you cover the time passage of years? If it's a musical biography, you can pick a hit song from the period—for example: play "You Make Me Feel So Young" over Sinatra's romance with Mia Farrow.

Montages of current events from TV news or newsreels can be used to transition your audience from one time period to another. It is important that your theme and story carry over strongly from one time period to the next, or you will have to re-engage your audience all over again every time you jump to a later date.

5 Changing partners is dangerous. When your story covers a great length of time, and you need to take a character from one age to another, it is very dangerous to change actors playing the protagonist in mid-movie. *Angela's Ashes* is an example of this problem. Just as the audience gets caught up in the plight of young Frankie, with no warning a complete stranger, a couple of years older, pops into a scene. People are calling him Frankie. And the little guy we loved and were rooting for has disappeared completely and never comes back. This can alienate an audience, so be careful as you structure your story. Try to find a way to tell the story so that one actor can play the protagonist all the way through if humanly possible.

Am I saying that if your main character goes from age 14 to 30, you should try to make it 18 to 28 just so one actor can play it? Yes. If you can do that without damaging your story too much, I suggest you do it. Many things can be accomplished with makeup or digital effects, but a human actor can only stretch so far. Work within an actor's limits whenever possible.

At the end of *Billy Elliot*, a whole new actor is introduced to play Billy at 25, now a professional ballet dancer. This was not a problem for the audience, because we got to stay with our child actor all the way through the story. The end is really just a tag, sort of a visual version of the crawl that tells us what happened after the movie ended. This actor doesn't finish the story for Billy. He's just a visual aid and a lovely one.

There have been movies in which actresses have played age 12 to adulthood. Sissy Spacek in *Coal Miner's Daughter* and Diana Ross in *Lady Sings the Blues* are two that spring to mind. They both won Best Actress Oscars for these feats. But they didn't play age 12 for long. As you structure your story and write your script, never lose sight of the fact that an actor will have to play it. It often helps if you can picture your favorite casting choice playing the scenes as you write them.

6 Time management devices. There are a few literary devices that can sometimes help:

Book Ends. This is where you start and end at the same period in time—flashing back for the bulk of your story, then coming back to the present at the end. *The Green Mile* is an example of this device. *The Princess Bride* with its story-telling device is another.

Time Jumps. The movie *Same Time Next Year* told the story of a couple meeting for a weekend affair once a year, but used the device of only showing us one scene for every five years. Once the audience got used to the five-year jumps, it was a lot of fun to watch.

Flashbacks. If you need a piece of the story to have happened in the past and you want to dramatize it (rather than explaining it), you can have a flashback scene. These have, however, become somewhat passé or old-fashioned. Here are a few tips on how to make flashbacks work:

a) Don't use them for purely expositional reasons. Find another way to cover your needed exposition.

b) If you're going to do flashbacks, you have to introduce the device at least once within the first 20 minutes, or it will be jarring when it occurs later.

c) Short flashback shots of images can be used to fill in clues, as when a character begins to put the pieces of a puzzle together. (See the last 20 minutes of *The Usual Suspects* for a good example of this working well.)

d) You can also do audio flashbacks, in which the character just hears something that happened in the past rather than showing it.

e) Don't show a character's face "remembering"—and then flash back to the memory. This is corny and rarely works. Same thing is true of showing a character sleeping, then using a dream sequence as flashback. That's even cornier.

7 The ticking clock. How many times have we seen the digital clock on a bomb ticking backwards toward zero? It is a favorite device for the third acts of action movies. You don't have to literally use a clock on screen, but sometimes it works. And what would a sports movie be without the final minutes of the game ticking down?

There is a famous story about the rough cut of *High Noon*, a classic western starring Gary Cooper and Grace Kelly—a film that takes place in a short time frame. The story goes that director Fred Zinnemann was working with his editor in the cutting room, and the rough cut was not very exciting. They came up with the idea of repeatedly cutting to shots of the clock on the wall ticking closer and closer to noon, when the big shootout would take place. It worked great, and the tension in that film builds perfectly.

8 Going backwards. Occasionally filmmakers have experimented with reversing the order of time. This has been tried occasionally by intellectual writers (Harold Pinter's *Betrayal* or Stephen Sondheim's *Merrily We Roll Along* are two examples). But while it may be interesting intellectually, emotionally it is usually a downer. It's depressing, after seeing how people have turned out cynical or corrupt, to go back and see how idealistic and fine they were in their youth.

Memento is a remarkably original film that successfully tells a story in reverse chronological order, beginning with the ending and moving backwards toward the beginning. The premise is this: A man with no short-term memory, because of brain damage from a head injury, is trying to solve his wife's rape and murder. By unraveling the story backwards, the audience is continuously thrown into the same disoriented state that the protagonist lives in. It works brilliantly. Rent it, if you missed it. (A cautionary note, however: Don't try writing one of these yourself until you have two or three scripts under your belt. This kind of structure is even more complex than it seems.)

This reverse gear worked great as a comedic device in the "Backward Episode" of *Seinfeld*. Knowing the future put the audience ahead in the joke on the hapless characters, and it was hilarious.

9 Playing hopscotch. Occasionally there have been fascinating artistic films covering a large span of history, with a series of separate but connected stories. *The Red Violin* was a notable example of this. The violin itself became the main character. But the movie also used the book-end device repeatedly to anchor the story to the modern-day auction of the violin, getting the audience interested in its fate. Needless to say, it is a hard approach to pull off. The danger is that each time you jump, the audience will be disappointed to leave characters and a setting that it has invested in. Viewers will resent being yanked out and dropped into a strange new time, and will need to orient themselves all over again.

If you want to keep an audience interested in your movie, let them know *when* they are and *when* they're headed to—and then get them there in as short a time as possible. Feel the need for speed!

CHAPTER 9

Structuring Scenes: Decapitating the Brontosaurus

Like the screenplay as a whole, each scene also needs structure: a beginning, middle, and end. And each scene needs some sort of conflict to drive it, if you want it to work. The conflict doesn't have to be overt. It can be subtle, but with no conflict, scenes just lie there, limp.

How long should a scene be? A scene can be as short as an eighth of a page or as long as five pages. Occasionally, you may need to have an even longer scene, such as a big climactic scene or scene sequence in which your story wraps up or in which the story explodes. A final battle scene, action sequence, or courtroom trial may require more than five pages. The Normandy invasion sequence in *Saving Private Ryan* was more than 20 minutes long. But it is an exception. I wouldn't suggest going that far unless you happen to be Steven Spielberg hitting his 20th home run. There is also a wonderful long scene at the end of *Moonstruck* in which all the subplots come together at the family breakfast table.

But as a rule of thumb, never let a scene go to ten pages. Ten pages is, after all, one-twelfth of your entire movie. Rarely can a single scene support that much weight. Try to keep your scenes five pages or less.

The brontosaurus. If you were to draw a diagram of them, many scenes would tend to have the natural profile of a sleeping brontosaurus. They start out at the head with low energy, they build in the middle to the important incidents or dialogue, and then they wind down again and peter out at the tail.

Example: The first draft of a scene might start as a car drives up to an apartment building. John parks, gets out, walks up to the building, pushes the buzzer. Harry's voice answers over the intercom. John identifies himself, and Harry buzzes him up. John goes up the stairs, and Harry opens the apartment door. John goes in. Harry closes the door. He offers to take John's coat. John takes his coat off. Harry offers John a drink. John declines. Harry offers him a seat. John does or doesn't sit. Then they get to the point of the scene. John tells Harry that their friend Alec is dead.

That paragraph above is just the head of the brontosaurus. A monster, isn't it? You need to whack it off. Just cut it and toss it. Try starting the scene here:

INT. HARRY'S APARTMENT. DAY.

Harry looks stunned as John stands in front of him still wearing his overcoat. Harry begins to pace.

> HARRY
> Are you sure? Did you see
> him dead? Because you know
> Alec...

> JOHN
> I saw him.

Harry stops in his tracks.

> HARRY
> Son of a *bitch*. Does she know?

> JOHN
> No.

Harry turns without another word and bolts out the door.

This is the body of the brontosaurus. It is the meat of the scene. This you keep. But you also need to lose the tail. You know what I mean: the part where Harry runs down the stairs. John goes out and closes the door behind him. Harry comes out of the building. John comes out of the building. John gets back into his car and drives off. You don't need this, so don't keep it. One of the ten commandments of screenwriting is: "When in doubt, cut it out."

Why it's important to cut heads and tails. When you start at a low-energy place (the drive-up, walk-up, entering-a-room brontosaurus head), you have to build energy from nothing. It's hard work. Then once you get the scene cooking, if you let all the energy wind down to low again, it means the next scene will have to work twice as hard to get the energy up again. It's like starting each time from a parked car, always trying to get it up to speed.

By cutting into a scene when the energy is still high from the last scene, and cutting out before it sags, you have a real advantage as you cut into the next scene. You start off with higher energy. The next scene can then build on that—until your entire movie is gaining energy and momentum.

It's like jumping from one train car to the next when all of them are moving forward together. This is what we are aiming for: scripts that are page-turners. Movies in which there is no moment that allows somebody to run to the restroom without missing something good. Not a wasted scene, nor a wasted moment.

Buttoning a scene. One way to tell how good a screenwriter is: How well does he or she get out of scenes? Do they know the perfect moment to cut on? Do scenes lose momentum and wind down, or do they end crisply and cut—*bang!*—right into the next?

Harry bolting out of the room is the "button" of the scene above. It's a button because it has a little bubble of energy. It is a quick, contained action. A button can also be a punch, a funny line or action. It can be a question. Begin to watch scenes on TV and in films more carefully, looking for the buttons. Not all scenes have them, of course. But the best screenwriters know how to button every scene.

A button can be learning a key piece of information. In the climax of *The Empire Strikes Back*, Luke Skywalker is battling Darth Vader with light sabers. Vader cuts off one of Luke's hands and has Luke dangling on a precipice by his other hand. When Darth Vader tells Luke at this moment that he is Luke's father, this is a major reveal. Now, the writer could have had Vader deliver the line—they look at each other . . . and cut. Does that seem a little incomplete to you? There would be unanswered questions left hanging. Is the fight over? How does it finally end? And does Luke believe him?

How the scene actually ends is with a button. In this case, it's an action. The moment after Vader reveals this information, Luke, who is hanging over a thousand-foot drop by his one remaining hand, looks up at Darth— and then lets go, falling backward into the vast abyss. This action tells the audience that Luke believes Vader is his father. Period. End of scene. This is the effect a button should have. It is the period that ends the scene cleanly and decisively.

The most important button is the last moment of the movie. We'll get into this in detail in Chapter 22, "Writing a Great Ending."

Multi-task scenes (combining scenes). New screenwriters tend to have one scene for each thing they want to have happen. As you gain experience, you begin to realize that several things can happen in the same scene. For example, we could have had three separate scene cards for the "High School Cinderella" story with these scenes:

a) Show Courtney working at fast food place. Hates her job.
b) Courtney meets prince and they have a moment.
c) Show stepsisters being mean to her.

However, it is not hard to see that one scene could have combined all three: Courtney is working in a burger place; the prince comes in and she waits on him. Then her sisters show up and ruin the moment by being rude and obnoxious to her. This is not only economical, but it makes a more interesting scene.

Mini Scene-Cards. One last tip to help you master writing individual scenes is creating mini Scene-Cards. These come in handy if a scene is unwieldy, complex, or hard to organize—like the summation to the jury of a complicated case. A battle scene or chase sequence. The detective filling in the family on the solution to the murder mystery. A school picnic. For these kinds of scenes in which a lot of things have to happen and many things have to be said, I use the following technique.

I write the key pieces of information, dialogue, and actions on small Post-its (1" by 1.5" size) and then lay them out until the scene builds to the climax I want it to, with its button at the right moment. Then I stick the Post-its onto the cardboard back of a legal pad. That way, I can stand the mini-storyboard beside my computer and type straight from it. This technique makes even extremely complex scenes workable.

One of the best things about writing individual scenes is that they are manageable little pieces—that add up to a movie. Even the toughest scene can be written in a day!

Scene Checklist

✅ Is this scene necessary to the story?

✅ Does it have conflict? Can it have conflict?

✅ What is the purpose of the scene? The intention? The heart?

✅ How late can I come into this scene?

✅ How early can I get out of the scene?

✅ Can I accomplish more than one thing in the scene?

✅ Can I combine this scene with another scene?

✅ How can I button this scene?

✅ Would a mini-storyboard help?

CHAPTER 10

Set-Ups and Pay-Offs

We now get deeply into the mechanics of the craft and look at how the storylines get woven together smoothly until it all seems effortless, as if it unfolds naturally. All of the big moments in a screenplay require the right set-ups in order to have impact. Funny, sad, scary, or outrageous moments all need to be properly set up. This is a highly manipulative art form, and Set-Ups and Pay-Offs are two of the primary tools screenwriters use to make the manipulation machinery run.

Why do we remember for half a century the line, "Play it, Sam," from *Casablanca*? Because the set-up was very strong. Bogart's character (Rick) had made it emphatically clear that his piano player Sam was never, under any circumstances, to play "As Time Goes By." His statement admonishing Sam was Set-Up #1. Then we see the flashbacks of the romance with Ilsa (Set-Up #2) and finally Ilsa walks in and Sam plays it for her (Set-Up #3). By the time Rick buckles and asks Sam to play it, it is powerful for the whole audience. This is the Pay-Off. The song and the line both became indelible classics. If the movie had opened with Rick asking Sam to "play it again," it would have been just one more movie moment that slips by and is forgotten. This is an example of how the right Set-Ups can empower the important moment.

While subplots require three beats, set-ups have no such rule. You can have one—or as many as you need. At the end of *One Flew Over The Cuckoo's Nest*, the Chief lifts an enormously heavy marble shower block and hurls it through the windows and bars and uses this hole to escape. This is the powerful climactic section of this movie (coupled with Mac's death, it is the climax). It has only one set-up: the scene where McMurphy bets the guys he can lift it, but he can't even move it, no matter how hard he strains.

Not a fraction of an inch. This single set-up gives us all of the following in the pay-off:

a) We know it is extremely heavy, almost impossible to lift. So the Chief has found his real strength and his power.

b) Since Mac tried to do it and failed, Chief has taken up the torch and is completing Mac's mission for him.

c) The image left behind of the broken window and the gushing water from the broken pipes lets the legend of Randall McMurphy live on. The guys think Mac beat the system. Because this is the same act Mac tried to do and failed at earlier, his legend lives; it will continue to inspire these men and help them find their own power to resist the system, and Big Nurse, that is trying to destroy them.

That's quite a big payoff for one small set-up, isn't it? Sometimes it works this way. If you find the right set-up.

How To Do It Yourself

Here is a blow-by-blow example from one of my recent screenplays. We are going to open up the hood, take the engine apart, and figure out how it runs. This example shows how to use Set-Ups to help an audience believe something that is wildly outrageous. The more outrageous the pay-off, the more carefully, and in this case, subtly, you want to make the set-ups. It may require several of them to do the trick. And I do mean *trick*.

e-tickets is a kid-driven action/adventure screenplay. By the time I got to page 72, the three kids are in Paris, with the police after them, and with nearly unlimited funds. I wanted to write a scene where it's Lizzy's 16th birth-day. And her little brothers surprise her by fulfilling a fantasy of hers: They give her a Ferrari, which they use immediately for escape in a high-speed chase sequence. You may know that Ferraris (and all really great, expensive sports cars, as my son informs me) only come with stick shifts. Now, these are not that easy to drive. So it had to be believable that she could drive a Ferrari. I also wanted the scene be a total teenage-girl fantasy fulfillment sequence, worthy of vintage John Hughes' movies like *Sixteen Candles* and *Pretty in Pink*. So, let's take apart the machinery and see how it works.

I went back and filled in the Set-Ups, which were:

Page 5: While still at home in Seattle, eating pizza with her brother Jake, age 12:

>   JAKE
>   Are you really getting a car
>   for your birthday?
>
>   LIZZY
>   It's my sixteenth. What do
>   you think?
>
>   JAKE
>   I think it'd be an
>   interesting precedent.

Page 6: Dad pulls into the driveway in (you may have guessed it) a black Ferrari.

Page 7: When her Dad tucks her in and says goodnight, Lizzy asks "Can I practice driving your car again tomorrow?" (I have a 15-year-old daughter and such requests are normal and frequent.)

What we are trying to accomplish with these Set-Ups is to sneak them by an audience so it doesn't realize it's being set up. These beats we are inserting should seem to be normal and real, sliding right by without drawing attention to themselves.

Page 22: In New York City, at the famous F.A.O. Schwarz toy store, on a quest for a Ouija board, they're scanning the shelves of toys:

>   JAKE
>   What do you want for your
>   birthday, Lizzy?
>
>   LIZZY
>   Nothing they sell at F.A.O.
>   Schwarz.

                    JAKE
So? *What?*

                    LIZZY
I want a guy that looks like
Jude Law to dance with me and
kiss me while a band plays
"Unchained Melody."

                    JAKE
And a baby blue Ferrari.

                    LIZZY
Absolutely.
        (sees Ouija board)
There it is.

Page 69, in Paris now, Jake goes into an exclusive jewelry shop and pulls
out a 10-carat ruby (another thread of the story). He tells the proprietor, "I
need to trade it for this. And I need it delivered." He hands the man a piece
of folded notebook paper with instructions on it.

Page 71. EXT. SIDEWALK CAFÉ. PARIS. NIGHT. The three kids (Lizzy,
Jake and Jordy, age 10) sit at a table in an outdoor café at night beside the
river Seine. It's a gorgeous, romantic setting, but things are not going well
for our kids on the run. They have had to flee their hotel when the police
showed up looking for them. In fact, a mercenary villain is watching them
from across the street right now.

Lizzy seems a little down. She excuses herself to go to the ladies' room.
And here is the scene:

                    JORDY
What's wrong with her?

                    JAKE
Do you know what day it is?

                    JORDY
Absolutely no clue.

JAKE

It's Tuesday. It's Lizzy's
sixteenth birthday.

JORDY

Oh. She was supposed to
have a big party.

JAKE

I know. So be nice to her.

JORDY

I'm always nice.

JAKE

Go give this to the guy with
the violin.

Jake gives Jordy a piece of paper folded together
with a hundred-franc note. Jordy goes. Lizzy comes
back and plops down in her chair.

LIZZY

It's hopeless.

JAKE

Look on the bright side. We
got to see Paris. We had an
adventure. And it's not over
yet. Anything could happen.

A BABY BLUE FERRARI convertible with the top down
pulls up at the curb in front of them and an
extremely handsome young man steps out. He looks a
little like Jude Law, in fact. Lizzy's eyes are riveted on him.

LIZZY

Oh my God. It's my car! And
look at the guy driving it.

At that moment "Jude" spots Lizzy, smiles and walks
right over to her. He reaches out and takes her hand,
gently pulling her to her feet as the STRING QUARTET
begins playing "Unchained Melody." Lizzy feels like
she is in a dream. She lets herself be led to the

sidewalk beside the river where the young man dances with her. Jordy sits back beside Jake and they grin as Lizzy and Jude dance.

Somewhere in the distance SIRENS can be heard. They may even be coming closer.

As the song ends, Jude kisses Lizzy romantically.

> JUDE
> Happy Birthday, Lizzy.

He hands her the keys to the Ferrari. She shrieks! And suddenly the SIRENS are here! French police cars pull up all around them. All three kids run to the Ferrari. Lizzy climbs in with the keys and starts the engine which ROARS to life. Jake and Jordy squeeze into the passenger seat.

> LIZZY
> I can't drive this!

> JAKE
> What do you mean? Dad's been
> teaching you to drive his!

> LIZZY
> I know, but I suck at it! I
> don't want to wreck the gears.

> JAKE
> Drive!

And Lizzy throws it into first and lays rubber as she hits the gas, narrowly missing the cop cars, running over the sidewalk, almost going off the edge into the river, then rocketing off down the boulevard. And the chase is on.

Okay, did you believe that this could happen? Was it fun? Even with all the Set-Ups pointed out? This is how the screenwriting engine runs. Just for fun, and to make it more believable that they would beat the cops, I added yet one more Set-Up and Pay-Off.

On the plane from New York to Paris, Lizzy masquerades as the boys' mother, using their mom's passport. When the steward comes around with the liquor cart, she asks if there is a drink limit. They're flying first class (on e-tickets, naturally) and he says, no, there's no limit. So she orders about eight miniature liquor bottles, all different colors and shapes. She tucks them in her purse, because "they're cute." During the chase scene, while Lizzy's driving, Jake pulls the little liquor bottles out of her purse and with Kleenex and a lighter, makes miniature Molotov cocktails and throws them out of the car so that they make fireballs in the road behind them. Are we having fun yet?

This is how the game is played. Once you know the effect you want to have on your audience, you work out ways to set things up—subtly if possible, believably if at *all* possible—so that you get the pay-offs you are after.

CHAPTER 11

Screenplay Format

Many of you may be already familiar with the basics of screenplay formatting. You can skip over parts you already know—but there may be a few new tricks you haven't picked up elsewhere. Have you ever needed to figure out how to format song lyrics? Intercut a phone scene? Format a montage? How about Superimposing and Voice-Overs?

Learning to format a script may seem like a huge pain in the neck when you first begin writing screenplays, but after awhile it becomes simple and automatic.

Basic Format

Paper and binding. Use plain white 20-pound typing or copier paper, 8½″ by 11″. Have it three-hole punched. Bind the script with brass brads or "script screws" (also known as "Chicago Screws"), which are available at many writing supply stores. These are also used for holding leather together and can be bought at tack shops where riding equipment is sold, or at leather-working supply stores.

Title page. Should have the title about 3″ from the top of the page, centered. Then beneath it: "An Original Screenplay by Your Name Here." If it is not an original screenplay, you need to say "Screenplay by You, from a Story by Your Brother," or whatever is the case. At the bottom right-hand corner of the title page, put your contact information: your agent's name or your own name, address, phone number, e-mail, fax, or all of the above. This is so they can find you if they love it.

Registration information. You should register your script with the Writers Guild of America (see Appendix F). I recommend that you write on the back of the title page, at the bottom, in fairly small print, "Registered WGA" (but no registration number, and *no date*). Protect your script. If they look for this indication, they will see it is registered. But don't plaster it across the title page. Paranoia is one of the surest tip-offs of amateurism. Be subtle.

No dates / no draft numbers. You wouldn't believe how fast things get old in Hollywood—faster than milk in your refrigerator. They invariably want only the newest and hottest. Not something from last week, or, God forbid, last *month*! So don't date your script. And don't ever say "First Draft" or even "Fourth Draft." To raise the question: "Why is this author sending me a first draft?" is bad. Even worse is: "Why isn't this script better after four drafts?" It's a no-win situation. Don't do it.

Page numbers. Top right-hand corner. Do not put your name on every page (as is common for book manuscripts). Title page is unnumbered, and the first page of the screenplay is page one.

Do not number scenes. This is done only to the shooting script just prior to the shoot. Spec scripts should never have scenes numbered.

Font. Screenplays must always be in Courier or Courier New font, size 12. This is standard. One page of a screenplay in Courier 12 equals one minute of film. Page counts are used for both budgeting and scheduling. If you turn in a script using a different font or type size, it will not look like a professional screenplay and will probably never be read.

Spacing. Scripts are single-spaced. Double-space between dialogue and action (i.e., one empty line-space between lines of type.) Triple-space between scenes (i.e., two blank lines before the next slug-line or heading).

Use present tense. Screenplays are written in present tense, in a direct, crisp style. Active sentence structure is preferable to passive. (Don't say:

"There was a man standing on the corner." Better: "A man stands on the corner.")

Page margins. Leave 1″ margins on top, right, and bottom. Use a 1.8″ to 2″ margin on the left—to accommodate three-hole punching. If the left margin is only 1″, it is hard to read once the script is bound together with brads or script screws.

Formatting Dialogue

Name of the character speaking. This goes in all-capital letters, beginning at the center of the page (not centered).

Dialogue. The lines of dialogue should extend about 12 characters to the left of the name and an equal distance to the right. Use script-formatting software if you like. Most word-processing programs have built-in software that will let you set up wrap-around columns of dialogue. (Most let you modify and customize shortcut keys as well.)

Parentheticals. These should start about 5 spaces to the left of the name.

In other words, your dialogue should look like this:

```
                    JOHN
                (seeing him)
        What are you doing here? I
        told you to stay in the car.
```

You can use parentheses for small actions by the actor who is speaking the lines. Example:

```
                    JOHN
        No thanks.
                (lights cigarette)
        I don't smoke.
```

Never put an action, as a parenthetical line, into the dialogue of any actor other than the one speaking.

Do not do this:

>   JOHN
>   Who the hell are you?
>   (Al hands him gun)
>   Am I supposed to say thanks?

Al won't hand him the gun. Al won't even *know* about the gun. Actors don't read each other's parentheses. Only put action into the dialogue performed by the actor speaking the line. For the above, you'd have to write it like this:

>   JOHN
>   Who the hell are you?

Al hands him a gun.

>   JOHN
>   (Continuing)
>   Am I supposed to say thanks?

Yes, it takes up more space, but at least this way John actually gets the gun.

No hyphenation, abbreviations, or numerals. In dialogue, use no abbreviations. Do not break a word with a hyphen. And spell out numbers.

Wrong way:

>   JIM
>   Are you Dr. Conway in apart-
>   ment 5?

Right way:

```
                    JIM
          Are you Doctor Conway in
          apartment five?
```

If you had an address in dialogue of, say, "18763 Wilshire Boulevard," the actor would have to try to figure out whether he's supposed to say: "One eight seven six three." Or "eighteen thousand seven hundred and sixty-three." Or several other possible variations. Spell it out for actors.

Continuing dialogue. If you have a speech that runs over at the bottom of the page, you must format it like this and continue it on the next page. At bottom of one page:

```
                    JOHN
          I don't know what you think
                    (MORE)

                                   CONTINUED.
```

Top of next page:

```
CONTINUED.
                    JOHN (CONT'D)
          you're doing, but it ain't
          gonna fly here.
```

Note the word "continued" in caps at the bottom right of the first page and top left of the second. Use this if any scene continues from one page to another, even if the dialogue is unbroken. If the scene does not continue, don't use "CONTINUED."

Headings. All scene headings or slug-lines must begin with either INT. or EXT. INT. is the abbreviation of interior and can be the inside of a building or a vehicle. Or the inside of anything that would be built as a set and not an outdoor location (space ship, igloo, etc.). EXT. of course is exterior and is for all outdoor scenes.

After INT. or EXT. briefly state the location. No extra words or descriptions. JOHNSON KITCHEN. ARMY HELICOPTER. Keep it short and clear. The whole heading needs to fit on one line, if at all possible.

And finally DAY or NIGHT. Not dusk, dawn, afternoon, early morning. This is for the people who have to schedule the shoot. Is it closer to day or night? Pick one. Occasionally it is critical to your story that it be literally, exactly SUNSET. But for the most part, professional screenplays use DAY or NIGHT. Period.

Sound effects. Sound effects should be capitalized. These include sirens, ringing phones, etc. If you see an actor making the noise, it is not a sound effect. If you see an actor slam the door, for instance, you don't need to capitalize it. If he stomps off-screen and slams the door, it is a recording.

The same goes for dogs and babies. If a baby is crying in the scene, it is an actor. If it is a baby crying off-screen somewhere, it is a sound effect. Ditto for dogs.

For a reading (or selling) script, you can use this rule to support the effect you want. In other words, if it is a loud or startling sound effect, capitalize it. Like a GUNSHOT. But if it is a quieter effect, such as crickets chirping, wind gently rustling the leaves, etc., it might detract from the mood to have the CRICKETS CHIRPING. Looks like giant insects are about to attack, doesn't it?

Phone sequences. You're right in the middle of a suspenseful phone call and you have to keep interrupting the flow to go back and forth between the characters. (Endless INT. JOHN'S HOUSE., then back to INT. MARY'S HOUSE.) Here's the shortcut: Set up the first scene normally. Once you cut to the other end and set up that scene, you can just add (INTERCUT PHONE SEQUENCE) and continue to write the dialogue as if it were one master scene. Like this:

```
INT. LIGHTHOUSE. NIGHT.

Harry grabs the phone and punches in a number as the
storm rages outside the glass all around him.

                              CUT TO:

INT. OSPREY's NEST PUB. NIGHT.

Jake sits at the bar nursing a glass of stout, his
black rain slicker dripping with rain on the stool
next to him. When his RADIO PHONE RINGS he picks it
up. (INTERCUT PHONE SEQUENCE.)

                    JAKE
          Yeah?

Harry has to shout to be heard over the storm now.

                    HARRY
          Jake! It's breaking at thirty
          feet over the bar! What have
          you still got out there?

                    JAKE
          Did you say thirty? Thirty
          feet?
```

And so on. They can talk and do things or whatever you like. The director
will film both sides of the conversation until the call is over. He/she will
decide which side to show at each moment. You can't control that. It is usually based on performances. When the call is over, whichever character you
continue to describe is where the camera will finish out the scene. Once
they hang up, you're back in one scene only. You can't jump back again.

Foreign languages. What if James is stopped at the border by a group of
Russian soldiers who turn to discuss his papers among themselves?
Obviously, they speak Russian and you don't. Here's how:

```
EXT. BORDER CHECKPOINT. NIGHT.

The Russian soldiers turn and talk among themselves.
(They speak RUSSIAN, subtitled.)

                       IVAN
             His papers are in order.

                     CORPORAL
             Something's not right about
             this. What is he doing here
             this time of night?
```

As simple as that. Of course, you could leave out the word "Subtitled," and they will speak Russian with no translation. You need to write it so that the translators will know what to translate and the actors playing Russians will know what to play.

Song lyrics. You want to have a character start singing, like Tom Hanks in *Splash*, when he starts dancing around the fruit warehouse singing "Mr. Mango on my shoulder . . ." If you wrote the words to song lyrics as if they were regular dialogue, an actor might embarrass himself at an audition or "Table Read" by reading the words, "Why do birds suddenly appear, every time you are near?" and feel like an idiot when he suddenly realizes it's a song. So you do it like this:

```
                    DOROTHY
                   (singing)
             SOMEWHERE, OVER THE RAINBOW
             WAY UP HIGH
             THERE'S A LAND
             THAT I HEARD OF
             ONCE IN A LULLABY...
```

Try to break the lines where they break in the lyrics.

Montage Sequences. If a scene has live sound and dialogue, it is usually considered a scene, no matter how short it is. But if you have a montage sequence with music or narration over, and no "live sound," you don't need to set up every shot with a heading like a full scene. You can do it like this:

BEGIN COUNTY FAIR MONTAGE. (CALLIOPE MUSIC OVER)

THE FAIRWAY.

Tom and Becky make their way through the crowds.

COTTON CANDY BOOTH.

He buys her a gigantic pink cloud of cotton candy on a stick.

STRONG-MAN BOOTH.

On his third attempt, Tom swings the sledgehammer and RINGS THE BELL.

SIDESHOW.

Becky cringes at the sight of the man covered in pythons and grabs Tom's arm.

END COUNTY FAIR MONTAGE.

At which point you go to the slug-line of the next scene.

O.S. and V.O. Do you know the difference between O.S. and V.O.? O.S. means Off Screen. When a voice is O.S. the characters in the scene can hear it. Like a TV announcer or a guy hollering from the shower in the next room. V.O. stands for Voice Over, which means that the characters on screen can't hear it, as in narration, or hearing a voice while someone is reading a letter.

M.O.S. This means "mit out sound," and it has been in use since the birth of movie-making. One of the early German directors coined it. You use it when you have a scene with no sound. A silent scene. Put it after the heading on the slug-line: EXT. ROAD. NIGHT. M.O.S. The director Michael Mann has used silent car sequences to create eerie, nightmare-like tension from basically simple shots.

INT/EXT. The combination INT/EXT. is used rarely, but it is handy if you want a traveling shot that includes the actors in the car and live dialogue as well as the vehicle action and road. Like the Phone Sequence it helps you avoid constant slug-lines breaking up the flow. Example:

INT/EXT. CAR/HIGHWAY. DAY.

Mary grabs John's arm as he spins the wheel and the Porsche nearly flies off the cliff as it barely makes the hairpin turn at 90 miles an hour.

Superimpose. If you need to establish time or place with a superimposed title, you set up the basic scene heading, describe what's on-screen, then SUPERIMPOSE in caps, and the words you want on-screen centered, like this:

EXT. PENTAGON. WASHINGTON D.C. DAY.

Establishing Shot. Sunrise. SUPERIMPOSE:

"THE PENTAGON. 6:40 A.M."

Credit sequences. The opening credit sequence is usually left to the director, but if you have a good idea for the opening credits, you do it like this:

FADE IN.

EXT. NOVA SCOTIA COASTLINE. DAY.

(BEGIN MAIN TITLES) Then describe the scenes, use several headings if you like, then when you want to end the credits, add the words: (END MAIN TITLES.)

Script length. Never turn in a script shorter than 90 pages or longer than 129 pages. The exception is for comedies or animated films, which are shorter: 90 pages for the former and as little as 75 for the latter. For animated films, the cost-per-minute is too great to make them truly "feature length," but kids' attention spans are shorter, so the shorter length has become standard practice.

Camera directions. Never say "We see" or "Camera sees." *We* are not in the movie and neither is the camera. Don't use camera directions. It is the director's job to decide what shots he will use. They are offended when writers dictate these things. You don't need to end scenes with DISSOLVE TO, CUT TO, or FADE OUT, unless you want it for a particular effect. Use FADE IN only at the very beginning and FADE OUT at the very end. Never use ANGLE ON unless it is the only way to reveal a piece of story information. Example: Two people are having a drink at a small table. "ANGLE TO INCLUDE the man listening behind the door."

Capitalizing a character's name. The first time a character appears in the whole script (not in every scene), capitalize his whole name—unless his part is so small that he has no dialogue (which means the part will be played by an extra, not an actor). They use the capitalized names to count how many actors they need to hire.

In other words, "A COP steps in" means he says something. "A Cop steps in" means he doesn't talk. If a character has more than three lines, it would be nice to give him a name, for instance "Sam" instead of "Old Man." Don't forget some poor actor is going to have to say, "I played an old man in that movie." How much better for his actor's ego to be able to say, "I played Sam."

Screenwriters need every advantage they can get when they're starting out to break into Hollywood. Delivering your script in professional format is one advantage you can easily give yourself.

PART TWO

The Heart

Once you have a well-constructed spine, it's time to get the blood pumping. Now we begin the writing process. You've done the intellectual structuring; it's time to let go and let yourself be swept away by your "Wild Mind," as Natalie Goldberg calls it. Let the good times roll.

See the movie in your head and write it down as fast and as clearly as you can. Let the voices speak to you. Let the magic happen. This is, of course, a completely Right Brain process. Fortunately, once you've done the earlier Spine work, the structure becomes programmed into the subconscious, and you will usually stay more or less on track. Don't try to control your writing too much or lock it inflexibly into the structure. Trying to control the natural freedom of your creative heart will often stop the flow and stunt the writing process. Let it go. Don't worry if it goes off on its own.

It will usually circle back and give you more than you hoped for. What looked in skeleton form like a Great Dane may turn out to be a lion. Let it find its own life and run, rage, sing, and soar. Let it be a horrendous, bloody, explosive mess if it wants to be. Don't be afraid of it. This is the time for all of life to break loose. Breathe life into it now. Tame it later.

CHAPTER 12

Switching to the Right Brain

Having been heavily in Left Brain mode until now, we may find it tricky to switch to the right, creative brain to begin writing the script. Ideally, the Left Brain will be so confident by virtue of having structured and scene-carded the whole story that it will feel that "any fool" can fill in the gaps. Hopefully, the general will march off the field—leaving the soldier free to pull out his easel and become a painter.

Finding the Doorway into Your Movie

It can sometimes be hard to find the doorway to the script—the secret passageway leading from the harsh daylight of outline and format into that dark theater where your movie plays for the first time for an audience of one.

Here is one example from my own experience of how this shift can occur. In 1998, I was writing a historical docudrama for CBS, a true story from the Civil War about a wealthy woman in Richmond, Virginia, who became Ulysses Grant's best spy behind enemy lines. Her name was Elizabeth Van Lew, and the project was called *Crazy Bette, the Madwoman of Richmond*. I had done all the research, made my cards, structured it all. The network had even approved the outline. Now to begin writing. And I was stuck.

I had great material. This woman was in her early forties, had never married, so that when her father died she would inherit his slaves and be in a position to free them. (If she had married, they would have gone to her husband.) She was a true abolitionist, with the courage of her convictions. When the war broke out she used an old school friendship with a woman who was now Mrs. Jefferson Davis, first lady of the Confederacy, to gain access to the Confederate White House. She even placed Mary, a young black woman, there as a loaned-out lady's maid, having taught her to read and write from childhood. Mary, her surrogate daughter, became her partner in espionage. Between the two of them, they managed to get information from Davis's own private desk directly to General Grant. They were never caught. Elizabeth's cover was feigning mental illness. Thus the title *Crazy Bette*.

So, great material. Great character. Let's go to it. But I was stuck.

I knew it had to start with the War breaking out. Without the War, there's no problem. And if there's no problem, there's no story, right? But I just couldn't see it. None of the scenes I had planned worked for me as an opening scene. They just didn't feel right or look right. They might have seemed like good ideas to my Left Brain, but my creative Right Brain just wasn't inspired by them. I didn't want it to start with military movements or battles. Or newspaper headlines. Or announcements of war from the pulpit in church. None of that felt right. It all felt like cliché Civil War movie stuff.

I also didn't want to start with the commonplace women-at-home, slice-of-life, meet-the-household, everyday-life stuff. Cooking, cleaning, serving dinner, *dull!* This story was different. It was unique and needed to be told beautifully from the very first shot. So what could it possibly be?

My analytical Left Brain got disgusted and said, in essence, "Well, I've given you all my best, brilliant ideas—and if you don't like any of them, then you're on your own." And it left me to stew about it. I kept looking and couldn't see anything. Vision—visual imagery—is the best way to make the shift to the Right Brain. You have to see it in your mind before you can write it on the page. I saw nothing.

Then, finally, an image appeared. It was of the house. The Van Lew mansion above a sloping lawn on Church Hill in Richmond. Huge oak trees spreading on either side. Seen from directly in front, a perfectly symmetrical image. Just a house. A building. That's all. But I stayed with it and slowly my mind's camera began to move in on a window, and through that window I saw a man lying in bed, his wife bending over him on one side and his daughter, Elizabeth, on the other. Like two angels, still a symmetrical image, helping him leave his earthly cares behind.

Once I had seen this, I could begin to write. Wherever this image came from, I knew that once it was written down, the rest would unfold. The way the Right Brain works is like pulling a magic thread. You don't have to know all of it, just the next sentence. If you trust what you see, and write it down, the rest will follow. E.L. Doctorow once said that writing a novel was like driving across the country at night. You could only see as far as your headlights, but you could make the whole journey like that. *This* is like that.

Here is the opening sequence of *Crazy Bette, the Madwoman of Richmond*, written by the Right Brain:

```
EXT. VAN LEW MANSION. DAY.

SUPERIMPOSE:

        RICHMOND, VIRGINIA. JANUARY 8, 1861

The finest neighborhood in the city of Richmond in
the last elegant days of the Antebellum Era, the Old
South as it once was. On a hill stands a grand old
mansion with massive white pillars across the wide
front veranda. It is possibly the grandest house in
old Richmond, with the exception of the Governor's
Mansion nearby, (soon to become the Confederate White
House).

Perfect lawns. Huge spreading oak trees dripping with
Spanish moss. The house looks down the hill out onto
the James River and the waterfront docks and ware-
houses.

CLOSE ON an upstairs window of the house. Through it
a four-poster bed and an old man, MR. VAN LEW, dying.
His wife and daughter sit on either side of him. PUSH
IN as he breathes his last breath. ELIZABETH, his
daughter, a strong, intelligent woman of 43, leans
down to kiss his hand. Her mother, MRS. VAN LEW (62),
is a dignified, intelligent woman. She gently closes
her husband's eyes and puts her cheek to his as the
warmth slowly leaves him.
```

INT. STUDY. DAY.

Elizabeth, wearing a black dress, sits at her
father's desk writing out letters. Several envelopes
she has already finished lie before her. She finishes
another letter and carefully blots the ink before she
folds it. MARY comes in. She is a bright, pretty
black girl in her early twenties and carries a tray
of coffee, a sliced apple, small cakes.

                    MARY
          You need to eat something.

Elizabeth is so involved in what she is working on
that she doesn't even glance at the tray.

                    ELIZABETH
          Mary, I want you to ask
          everyone to meet with me in
          the drawing room.

Mary is not sure she understands.

                    MARY
          Everyone? There's no one
          here, Miss Elizabeth.

                    ELIZABETH
          John, Martha, Robert,
          everyone. Tell them to put
          aside whatever they are
          working on.

Mary is concerned and almost afraid at this. It seems
terrible and ominous in light of the master's death.

                    MARY
          Are you going to have to sell
          us off?

Elizabeth looks pained by the question and looks at
Mary with real sadness.

                    ELIZABETH
          No, Mary. I wouldn't do that.

Mary is greatly relieved at this. She nods and turns
to go.

> ELIZABETH
> (Continuing)
> And Mary? Have the children
> come as well. Even the
> smallest.

Mary nods and goes out. Elizabeth continues to write
out the letters in a neat and steady hand.

INT. DRAWING ROOM. VAN LEW HOME. DAY.

The family slaves are gathered in the drawing room,
five women and four men and half a dozen children
ranging in ages from a babe in arms to seven years
old. They all look afraid at being gathered in the
nicest room in the house. Elizabeth comes in with the
handful of envelopes. A couple of the younger men
look hopeful at the sight of the envelopes, hoping
for a bit of money possibly from the Master's will.

Elizabeth opens the door a bit wider and her mother
follows her in and stands silently behind her, sup-
porting what her daughter is about to do, as
Elizabeth turns to face them.

> ELIZABETH
> You all know that my father
> died this morning.

They murmur "Yes...God rest him," etc.

> ELIZABETH
> (Continuing)
> I loved and respected my
> father more than any person I
> have known in my life. But we
> had one point on which we
> parted ways. Now that he is
> gone, I am empowered to do
> that which I have longed to do
> since I was a small child. I
> have a document for each one
> of you, which is legal in any

                          state, certifying that from
                          this day you are free.

There is a gasp as this idea hits them. At first they
are not sure they understand, doubting that it can be
true.

                              ELIZABETH
                            (Continuing)
                    If you choose to stay with us,
                    you will be paid a fair wage
                    each week. And if you choose
                    to go, you go with our
                    blessings and with our thanks
                    for the faithful service you
                    have always given us.

She walks to each one of them, giving them the letter
with his or her name on it. Some of the women and a
couple of the men begin to cry as they take the letter. She says each name as she gives it, to try to
help them realize the moment and what is happening to
them.

                              ELIZABETH
                            (Continuing)
                    John, you are a free man.
                    Minnie, you are free. Ned,
                    you are free. Martha, you are
                    free. Will. Robert. Rose.
                    Sadie. Mary. You
                    are free.

It is a powerful moment for all of them. The baby
begins to cry and Elizabeth puts her hand on his
head, smiling.

                              ELIZABETH
                            (Continuing)
                    You, too, Georgie.

This is what happens when you let the Right Brain take you there and follow the thread to see where it leads you. Magic can happen. What the Right
Brain somehow knew was that this event was the beginning of Elizabeth's

real life. From this opening, the audience gets who she is and invests in her emotionally. The bonus is that when an actress reads an opening like this, she wants to play the part. Who wouldn't? She frees the slaves in the first five minutes.

Ways to Access the Right Brain

The senses. There are tricks and techniques that help us switch from analytical Left Brain to the creative Right. The key is usually in the senses. "What do you see?" is most often the key question. The other senses can also help get you out of the intellectual, logical brain.

> What do you hear? Loud music? Dishes banging in the kitchen?
> What do you feel in this scene? Is it eerie or silent?
> What kind of day is it? Is it dark and shadowed? Bright and sunny?
> What time of year is it? Blustery autumn? Icy winter? Sultry summer?

You circle around the thing, looking for details. Listening for clues. Sniffing it out until it begins to come alive and move on its own. That is the magic we are looking for. Here are some other tools for brain-switching that may help.

Soundtracks. Imagine what kind of music your movie should have—and go out and buy a CD or two that evoke that feeling. A movie soundtrack with a similar mood can help you get into the right space to write your own. When I was writing a Hallmark Hall of Fame that took place on a horse farm, I played the soundtrack of *The Reivers* because it had the feel of horse country, and because it's a great, inspiring soundtrack. Ken Burns' *Civil War* soundtrack kept me in period for *Crazy Bette*. What about your movie? Does it have a *Big Chill* Motown feel? Should it be filled with classic oldies like *Sleepless in Seattle*? Pick some soundtracks and try them out. Finding the right music can get you into the Right Brain.

Pin-ups. I've found pictures to be a great help getting me into my movies. When I was writing an Elvis miniseries, I had pictures of Elvis taped up all over my office. Working on a feature for Dreamworks about a lobster fisherman in Maine, I tore apart calendars from Maine and wrote surrounded by pictures of the landscape, fishing boats, and lighthouses. (A secret weapon is a substance called Goo Gone which takes the tape marks off afterwards and gives me more freedom to play without having to repaint.)

If having a particular actor in mind for a leading role helps me to hear the character's voice and see the performance in my mind, I will tear pictures of that actor out of magazines and put them up on the wall. Try to find a picture where the actor is dressed as closely as possible to the way your character would dress. It is worth investing $3 in a magazine just to get a great tear sheet that helps make your movie come alive.

Hearing voices. It is essential to be able to hear your characters talking to you. What would they say or not say? If you are writing about a real person, it may be easier. When I was writing a TV movie called *Eleanor, First Lady of the World*, I was able to get recordings from the public library of Eleanor Roosevelt speaking. I knew that the role would be played by Jean Stapleton, who has a very distinctive and familiar voice, but I couldn't write with Jean's voice in my mind. It had to be Eleanor's voice. Jean had to sound like Eleanor. Not vice versa. This one small act of playing Eleanor Roosevelt tapes in my car opened the whole screenplay for me. It made Eleanor real and personal, and the script unfolded magically and was written in less than a week. When magic happens, it is amazing. Do whatever you can to support that.

When I was writing Elvis, I rented all his movies, and I'd play half an hour of an Elvis movie during breakfast. It didn't matter if they were awful movies. It only mattered that I could hear Elvis talking in the room.

Usually, of course, we are writing about characters who are not based on real people or on people whose voices we can listen to over breakfast. I worked on a miniseries about billionairess Doris Duke and had a lot of trouble getting her character—until I imagined Lauren Bacall playing her. If I couldn't imagine Bacall's voice saying a line, it didn't go into the script. Amazingly, Lauren Bacall was ultimately cast and played the role. (I say amazingly because this almost never happens. What usually happens is that you hear Jason Robards' voice and they cast Mickey Rooney.) So I spent my evenings (not my writing hours) with Lauren Bacall movies playing on the box.

Study videos. Sometimes, particularly if I am writing in a style that is new to me, I'll watch movies that have the right tone, style, pacing, humor. I am impressionable. As a newly professional writer, I was hired to do a lot of script doctoring—that is, fixing and polishing other people's scripts, learning to write in their styles. So now, if I'm writing a romantic comedy, for instance, I'll watch *Notting Hill* over and over again, studying the rhythms in the language of the marvelous Richard Curtis, if that's the style I'm after for a particular project.

While writing *e-tickets*, I studied *Home Alone*. It was the level of reality I was after there and it gave me permission to take a few more pages at the beginning to set up a family and a reality base before taking off into the adventure. It made my script better. And it got me into movie mode—using my Right Brain. Being in the movie instead of staring blankly at a new document screen.

I often suggest that students do homework at the video store. Watch movies by people who have already mastered a particular voice, rhythm, or style that you are trying to master. (See Appendix D.)

Driving and the Right Brain. Have you noticed that while driving a car, creative ideas often come to you? I can sometimes see my movie play on the windshield as if I am sitting in a drive-in movie theater. Why is driving conducive to Right Brain takeover? I have a 15-year-old daughter with a learner's permit. She drives exclusively in her Left Brain, as all new drivers do. She endures a constant mental banter: Should I put on my blinker now? Am I going too fast? Do I have room to change lanes? If we spent our whole lives driving like this, we'd go nuts and road rage would be even more common. But usually, as we become experienced drivers, we let our Left Brains take a back seat and let the auto-pilot drive the vehicle—unless a potential problem appears, at which point the Left Brain storms back in and takes over. In the meantime, though, taking a drive can be a useful tool in getting us to muse on our story and letting the magic happen.

Taking a walk around the block can accomplish the same thing.

Tapping the Subconscious Mind. The subconscious is one of our greatest secret weapons. Many of you have had the experience of waking up and, still lying in bed, realizing that a story problem you struggled with last night has worked itself out while you slept. Somehow, you woke up knowing the solution. The Subconscious Mind is brilliant and will help you, but you can't control it or make it work for you. Most of the time it does its magic literally while you are asleep.

One simple way to harness this creative power is to look over your work before going to bed at night. Make a list of the scenes you want to work on tomorrow. If you are really stumped about some story glitch, write out the question or problem as concisely as you can on a notepad. Then sleep well. When you wake up in the morning, before you move or get out of bed, ask yourself again about the problem/scene/question. Then lie there and see if an answer isn't floating in your mind. Once you get it, get up and write it down. I have had students come back to me amazed at how well this simple process worked.

When I make a list of scenes I want to work on the next day, I get up the next morning and those scenes are ready to go. I type away and when I run out of gas and the fingers stall out, I'll look at my list and, sure enough, see that I have come to the end of those scenes I listed the night before. That's all that my Subconscious Mind had prepared.

If I get stuck mid-afternoon, I'll give up and lie down and take a ten-minute nap. I am one of those lucky ones who can lie down, be completely out for ten minutes, and wake up refreshed. Most of the time, after one of these brief blackout periods, I go back to the keyboard and the bump in the road begins to smooth out. The scene begins to work. It's kind of like the story of "The Shoemaker and the Elves." But it only works if you lay out the material. They don't make shoes from straw. But if you lay out good leather and a clear pattern, you may wake to see some mystifying, magical results.

There *is* a Subconscious Mind. It can be a valuable tool. Try using it.

CHAPTER 13

Falling in Love

We **tried an experiment** in my screenwriting class. We set out to discover what would happen if you treated your screenplay-in-progress like someone you had recently fallen in love with. What if you courted your story, wooed it, gave it your very best, and loved it madly? The results were extremely promising. Our conclusion was that if we were willing to throw ourselves into falling in love with our work, risking heartache, holding nothing back, the inner muses responded in kind. Magic happened.

Here are some of the things we came up with that worked great.

Atmosphere. Tailor your writing space to the piece you are working on. Surround your desk with a few related photographs, art postcards, or an appropriate talisman or two. For my Civil War story, I had old photographs of people and the city of Richmond, Virginia, circa 1863, on my desk, along with a few toy soldiers from that period.

Try limiting your reading and video rentals during these "love affair" weeks to things that inspire you on this project. Read authors who have the tone, style, or period you're trying to achieve in your own work, who speak the language and use the vocabulary you are currently working with. If you're writing urban teen, you might listen to rap. When I was writing about James and Dolley Madison, reading Jane Austen at night was the only thing that worked. Watch films that will inspire you to write well. Don't risk "garbage in/garbage out." Aspire to "greatness in/greatness out."

Dating. Set a precise date with your writing and then show up on time. Would you be late for a date with a person you were in love with? Give the same importance and attention to your writing. And make it quality time, not the end of the day when you're an exhausted zombie. Bring yourself to it at your best, whatever your peak performance hours might be.

The lunch date. I regularly take my script to lunch and while I'm eating I read it over, editing, polishing, adding things here and there. If you treat your project like good company and your companion of choice, see if it doesn't try to please you by being as lively and entertaining as possible.

Fidelity. While you are nurturing your love affair with one screenplay, other ideas will undoubtedly come to you and try to lure you away. The heat of passion is magnetic, and ideas will flock to you as moths to the flame. Tell them you're not available right now. You can jot down their names and phone numbers, but make it clear that you are devoted, right now, only to your one true love, the script you are writing.

Constancy. Most men know that no matter how much their lover may be a supportive, caring person, if they forget to call her for a few days, she's going to be angry. No lover likes to be ignored or forgotten. Try to pay attention to your script every day, even if only to reassure it that you're looking forward to spending time with it on Saturday afternoon. Don't let it be shuffled off under a pile of seed catalogs and golf magazines. If you want magic to happen, you have to treat your writing with respect.

If I try to carry this metaphor any further, it will be in danger of getting too cute, even for me. (I think it was Mel Brooks who wrote, "The pot of revolution was boiling over in the kitchen of France, staining the floor of history forever.") I know it's starting to sound silly, but those of us who have tried this experiment have had some exciting results. And we've had a great time. As in all matters of the heart, you have to take the risk and fall in love before magic will happen.

So check out all those ideas standing at the edge of the dance floor, pick out the smartest, best-looking one, and ask it to dance. Take it in your arms and let yourself fall.

CHAPTER 14

The Protagonist

The protagonist is the central character of your movie. The one driving the film. He or she is also our most important doorway into the experience of the movie. On some level the audience is the protagonist, identifying with this person most closely.

I am surprised at how often I read student scripts that make one of the three most common mistakes in shaping an effective protagonist:

Protagonist Mistakes

1 Protagonist as group. Scripts that have a group as protagonist, like *The Big Chill*, where we don't have one person to identify with, rarely engage us. Even if you have a group with a common problem, like being on the Titanic, there should be one character that the audience wants to identify with more than the others. Choose one. Focus on one central character. It puts us on that sinking ship, instead of watching it from a safe distance. (The reason we have to go as far back as 1983 to *The Big Chill* to find a memorable example of this is because that's about the last time a group-as-protagonist movie worked well.)

2 No clear protagonist. I read a screenplay recently about a group of high school students who decided to kill their unlikable teacher. There really was no protagonist. We not only didn't identify with them, we didn't *like* any of them. It is possible to like a movie in which you dislike every single character, but it is much harder. Having no clear protagonist gives the whole script a feeling of being held at arm's length, of looking at it through the wrong end of the binoculars. We see what's happening in the story, but we're not *in* it. Without the assistance of a protagonist, we have no way in. It becomes more like a fictional documentary; we are being shown a story in which we have no part. It's about as interesting as watching a horse race without placing any bets.

3 Picking the wrong protagonist. Sometimes a new screenwriter will actually think the wrong character is the protagonist. This throws the whole thing out of whack. For example, the writer might think the main character is the detective, when he is actually outside of the real story and has less stake in it than another character who is more deeply affected by the unfolding story.

How to Develop an Effective Protagonist

The one with the problem. The protagonist is the one who has the problem. Remember, without a problem, there's no story. If it's his story, it has to be his problem, right? So choose the character with the problem, put him or her at the center of the script, and tell that story. What is at stake for her? Be clear about the risks and invest the character in the plot.

Active not passive. In Chapter One, we talked about the danger of having a passive protagonist. This is a reminder: The protagonist has to be in the driver's seat. Not chasing after the car or tied up in the trunk.

Sympathy. Engaging an audience by creating a sympathetic character is the most common choice and a valid one, of course. If we care about the central character in the first ten minutes, we're in. The story's working. So, what can help us care about characters we've just met?

1. He may be clearly a decent, *good* person.

2. She may be the *underdog*, struggling against odds that are stacked against her (as in *Erin Brockovich*).

3. He may be very smart or very *talented* at what he does. We like people who are brilliant/strong/extraordinary in some way. Make a handsome movie star a math genius, dead shot, super spy, and an audience will immediately want to identify with that person.

4. She may be *passionate* about trying to achieve whatever her goal is. If the character cares passionately about something, it is easy for an audience to care about that person.

5. We may *feel sorry* for the guy. Hapless guys who get fired or dumped by their wives in the first ten minutes of a movie?—hey, we'll stick around and try to help them through it.

6. He may be so *unique*, quirky, enigmatic, or startlingly original that we want to find out what the deal is. Nicholson's obsessive/compulsive in *As Good As It Gets* is one of this category.

These choices offer enough ways to engage an audience with a protagonist that it shouldn't be hard to pick one or two. Let's look at some examples of problematic protagonists and how movies have dealt with them successfully.

Being John Malkovich is a very strange film based on a bizarre glitch in the time/space continuum. The central question is one that is really not an issue in any of our lives: "Is it better to be John Malkovich?" So why does the movie work? Why are we able, as an audience, to go with it? Because John Cusack's character is a protagonist that we can understand and identify with. He's a sad failure of a guy we can root for. He has a remarkable talent as a puppet maker and puppeteer, but the world has no use for his art. He can't make a living. His wife, while fine in some ways, has infested their home with all manner of ailing animals. And at the only job he can get, he has to bend over just to walk in the office. And the people there are even stranger than the creatures at home. We get who he is. We care what happens to him. And we'll follow him through this story no matter how weird it gets.

Memento is another example of an offbeat film with a protagonist that is hard to understand. We talked about it in terms of "The Ticking Clock" in Chapter 8. How do you get an audience to identify with a guy who is so unsure about himself and his own identity? First, our sympathy for his raped and murdered wife, whom he clearly loved deeply, is a doorway into the guy. Second, his passion to try to avenge her death pulls us into his story. And third, the reversed scene order makes us experience what he is experiencing simultaneously with him—in a very direct, if unsettling, way. When we cut to a scene where he is running down the street, asking himself "What's happening? Why am I running?" the audience is asking the same question. When he sees another guy running, he thinks, "Oh. I'm chasing a guy." And we think that, too. When the guy starts shooting at him, he realizes, "Oh no. He's chasing me." We get it as he gets it. Experientially, we are the protagonist.

The point is, no matter how bizarre and inaccessible the story is, if you give us a doorway into it, via a protagonist we can become, we'll go anywhere with you.

CHAPTER 15

Castable Characters

In this chapter, we'll address the crucial matter of writing roles that actors will *want* to play. If you are interested in making Independent Low Budget Art House Films this chapter is not really geared for you. If you want to break into Mainstream Big Screen Hollywood, it's essential.

Historically, there has always been a close affinity between dramatists and actors. Many of our greatest dramatic writers have been actors themselves. Shakespeare and Moliere were both actors. Actress Emma Thompson won the Academy Award for writing the screenplay to *Sense and Sensibility*. As a screenwriter, I almost always feel a close tie to the actors who breathe life into the characters that I have struggled for months to bring to life.

The practical reality of the movie business today is that to sell a script to Hollywood, it has to be castable. If the producers/agents/executives can't easily imagine that a star will want to act in your story, then it will probably never be bought, let alone made. If you have put a lot of energy into developing your characters and are alarmed by the idea that you might have to compromise your "Tom Joad" to fit a Tom Cruise, don't worry. Here is an easy checklist to help ensure that your script is "castable." The list may even make it a better script.

1 The list. Today a major motion picture costs a lot of money to make (we're talking tens of millions of dollars). There is a known list of bankable stars who can "open a picture." Which simply means audiences like them enough to come to a movie simply because, for instance, Julia Roberts is in it. The current list of the top box-office stars includes Tom Hanks, Russell Crowe, Jim Carrey, Robin Williams, Meg Ryan, Mel Gibson, Adam Sandler, Eddie Murphy, Cameron Diaz, Julia Roberts, Harrison Ford, Will Smith,

Tom Cruise, Jack Nicholson, John Travolta, Tommy Lee Jones, Brad Pitt, Pierce Brosnan, Nicolas Cage, Michael Douglas, Michelle Pfeiffer, and Sandra Bullock. This list changes as new movies hit big.

You need to at least be familiar with this list. It will change, depending on what movies have recently broken the $100 million mark. Keep an eye on up-and-comers like Heath Ledger, Hugh Jackman, and Angelina Jolie. They may be in the top 20 by the time this book is published. You can get an update on this list from John Willis's *Screen World* annual books. Or from *Premiere* magazine's yearly Hot 100 list. Or just keep an eye on which movies are huge hits. It's not hard to figure out. These are the actors that can get scripts made into films. In contrast, it's hard to sell a script if the main character is an albino dwarf. Even in the post-"Mini-Me" market, this is a tough sell. Write leading characters that stars can play and will *want* to play.

2 **Think 3-D**. Give the character more than one dimension. Don't write a stock hero/heroine. Actors want other levels to play; they want to tackle roles with internal conflict, something to make the character unique and interesting to play. Indiana Jones may have started out as a comic-book-type hero, but he also had a fear of snakes and was a wimp around Dad. Find surprising aspects of a character that will intrigue an actor.

3 **No specifics**. Steer clear of physical and age specifics. If you describe the person as six foot two, blond hair, blue eyes, 42 years old, and ruggedly handsome, you've put yourself into a pretty tight box. It might end up being your screenplay's coffin. How many stars in the top 20 box-office draws fit that description? Zero. None. This part is not castable.

On the other hand, if you describe him as ruggedly handsome, wearing a leather jacket and a beat-up fedora, with a whip slung over one shoulder—he could be any of them, from Mel to Tom to Harrison. Get the idea? Each star wants to feel like the part was written for him or her. So if she has brown eyes and you say blue, she is a little insulted. "Who was their first choice? Meg Ryan? Am I number 2? Number 11?" Slam. Pass. No go.

4 **How old do I look?** There is no way to win mentioning age. Even a generality like "early 40s" can be dangerous. Most stars in their late 50s to early 60s think they play in their early 40s. And the ones who are in their early 40s? They think they look 28, and of course some of them do. Just don't get specific about age.

5 **No names, please**. Never say "a Harrison Ford type" in describing a character. Harrison will think it's written for a B-list of his type. And everyone else will think it's for Ford. You end up with nobody.

6 **Give him/her an entrance**. When you describe the character the first time we meet him/her, make sure we know it is the main character. For example, don't introduce a group of five guys, but not reveal until a few pages later which one of them is the protagonist. We need to know right away. Make it clear. If you can give your character a great entrance or a wonderful character-defining moment in the first few pages, it will be to your advantage. When we meet Butch Cassidy, he is casing a bank and being charming and funny about it. An actor needs to be able to understand fairly quickly who the character is and if it's going to be worthwhile to read on. Stars work hard. They're tired, and they get scripts by the trunkload piling up on their patios. Make yours the one with the great character that hooks them in the first ten pages.

7 **Good dialogue**. Try to give your leads at least some of the best lines. Beware of giving the comic sidekick all the best laughs. This will definitely irritate your star. It is tempting sometimes, especially if your main character is one of those strong silent types, a man of few words. Don't forget it was Eastwood who said, "Make my day." And nobody but Schwarzenegger who said, "I'll be back."

8 **Duh**. Don't make the main character stupid. (Unless, of course, you're doing your *Rainman* or *Waterboy* farce.) The hero should not be behind the audience in figuring things out, or if he is, he shouldn't stay there for long. Nobody, especially an actor, wants to be perceived as dumb.

9 No (parenthetical directions)! Tell them what to say, but don't tell them how to act. Those little parenthetical directions—SAM: (angrily) What?!?—from the writer really annoy actors. I have seen actors flip through a script and cross out every single one without reading them before a table read. Only use parenthetical directions if the line would otherwise be unclear.

10 Where's my Oscar? You will give yourself a definite edge in the Hollywood Derby if your main character has at least one great scene which an actor can readily imagine being the clip they will show in the Oscars telecast just before they announce the winner of "Best Actor in a Leading Role." This award-winning scene can be any one of the following categories:

a) A Blow-up. Shirley MacLaine in *Terms of Endearment* screaming for someone to get her daughter some pain medication. Nicholson in *A Few Good Men* screaming, "You can't handle the truth!" Is there a moment where your character could lose it? Try finding it. And push it.

b) A Breakdown. Pacino almost blowing his brains out in *Scent of a Woman*. Jessica Lange in *Frances* or *Men Don't Leave*. Actors love to fall apart on screen.

c) A Freak-out. Brando shouting, "Stella!" Let's face it, hysteria is fun.

d) A Big Heroic Moment. Sally Field holding up the Union sign and stopping the mill in *Norma Rae*. Mel Gibson singlehandedly saving Scotland in *Braveheart*. Almost all stars want to be heroes.

e) A Terrific Physical Set-piece. Cary Grant being chased by Hitchcock's cropduster. Jeff Bridges standing on the edge of a ledge 100 stories up in *Fearless*. It doesn't hurt to give a little thought to what an actor's fantasy might be. Tom Hanks may have wanted to dance on that giant toy piano in *Big*. Try to imagine what they'd love to do in a movie and let them do it—if it can work for your story.

f) Words, Words, Words. If the character has a show-stopping speech or great dialogue throughout, actors are going to want to say those lines. It's one way to get to their hearts and minds both.

g) A Breakthrough. If your character can have a crisis of faith, make a leap, be redeemed, grow, transform, evolve, this is the best. Rick in *Casablanca*. Jack Nicholson in *As Good As It Gets*. It is the actor's ultimate trick, and what's wonderful about it is that it's not a trick at all. It's the real magic, and actors are hungry for it.

Ultimately, the most important thing you can do is to fall in love with the character yourself. If it's someone you love, chances are an actor will catch that, like a highly contagious, wonderful virus that will infect a star with that same passion.

CHAPTER 16

Surprises

What is bad screenwriting? I use soap operas as the ultimate example. Why? Because in a soap opera a character named Tiffany will say, "I am so furious at Todd. I'm going to go over there and give him a piece of my mind!" Cut to Todd's. The doorbell rings, Todd answers it and—guess what? That's right. It's Tiffany. And sure enough, she comes in and yells at Todd.

There are no surprises in soaps. In fact, the events that do occur come after months of painstakingly *unsuspenseful* buildup. When the Writers Guild goes on strike, the soaps are the only series that are not affected much. Actors have told me how during the strike the fans come in and write the scripts, the actors improvise a bit, and no one complains about loss of quality. Because there are no surprises. The fans know what's going to happen as well as the writers themselves.

As screenwriters, what we are trying to do is surprise the audience. It is the magic of sleight of hand. It is why *Pulp Fiction* was such a hit. It gave us set-ups that we have seen many times and made us expect certain events to follow others, and then took wildly unpredictable twists and turns. *Pulp Fiction* is raunchy and raw and ultra-violent, too much for many viewers. But looking beyond that to the story, it was one surprise after another.

Example: Bruce Willis, a boxer, takes money to throw a fight, doesn't throw it, and goes on the lam. We all know with complete certainty that this guy is going to end up dead or beaten to a pulp. But no. He ends up saving the life of the guy that's trying to kill him. And in the most shockingly surprising way.

Another scene: Two hitmen shoot a man in the back seat while driving in a car. The problem turns out not to be that they may get caught or killed themselves, but that the wife of the killer who owns the car will find it trashed and bloody and will divorce him. The whole frenzied clean-up action is to try to save the guy's marriage. These are cliche movie set-ups with wildly original consequences we haven't seen before.

Big surprises are so rare in movies that when they work they can make a hit out of an otherwise merely "pretty good" movie. *The Crying Game* was a good little story; it delivered a surprise so total and so skillfully played out (and so well kept by people who had seen the movie) that it turned a sweet little film into an Oscar contender. Likewise, *The Usual Suspects* had a great punchline—shown visually instead of told in dialogue, making it even stronger.

Another type of wonderful writing surprise comes when we think we know who a character is—and then a whole new and surprising layer of character is revealed.

One of my favorite examples is from *Five Easy Pieces*. Jack Nicholson is set up as a blue-collar oil-field worker, the type who thinks it's funny to pull a straw wrapper out of his nose. He and his equally grease-stained, hard-hat buddy get stuck in a traffic jam on the highway in their pickup. The traffic is at a standstill. No amount of drunken yelling helps. So Jack climbs up onto a flatbed truck in front of them to try to see what's going on up ahead. The furniture under the blankets emits a piano plink as he steps on a covered keyboard. He pulls the blanket off and finds an old upright piano and sits down at it. We expect "Chopsticks" or at best boogie-woogie. But this guy starts playing Chopin—and damned well. He gets so into it that when the truck starts moving, he doesn't even notice. His buddy yells at him to no avail as the truck carrying Jack and the piano takes an exit and heads off to God knows where.

Who is this guy and why is he working in an oil field? We don't have any idea, but we sure want to stick around and find out. We are surprised, delighted, energized by what we don't expect.

It is similar to the moment in *Shine* when schizophrenic David Helfgott sits down at the piano in a restaurant, and though we in the audience know he is a brilliant pianist, we hold our breaths, thrilled at how surprised those people are going to be when they hear this shuffling-and-drooling crazy rip into "The Flight of the Bumblebee." And the surprise does not disappoint. For my money, that is the best moment in *Shine*.

Years ago in a movie called *Rancho Deluxe*, a young Native American cowboy makes a pile of money rustling cattle. Driving a brand-new pickup truck, he goes home to see his father. His old man, played by Chief Dan George, takes one look at that shiny new truck, and we're sure he's going to jump his son for his life of crime. Instead he launches into a hilarious diatribe about how the pickup truck has been the downfall of their people. It's delightful.

I have saved my favorite for last. It is from a small English independent film released in 1999 called *Beautiful People*. Written and directed by Jasmin Dizdar, it is made up of a lot of separate stories and seemingly unrelated characters that, by the end, have pulled together into an amazing whole, utterly intertwined. Right around the halfway point, there is a scene sequence lasting around seven or eight minutes that completely blew me away. Here it is:

Contemporary London. A young skinhead, a junkie around 20 years old. He and two of his druggie friends are at the airport, passed out in the boarding lounge, waiting for their flight to Amsterdam, where they're going to buy drugs. They are so out of it, that when their flight is called, one guy is completely unconscious and the second has to half carry him onto the plane. The third, our guy, is so stoned he is sleepwalking. Shuffling across the tarmac toward the plane, he veers off course and ends up stumbling against a loaded pallet. Like a sleepy child, he lies down on it and pulls a tarp over himself.

The next thing we know, his pallet is loaded on a cargo plane and parachuted down to earth. The guy wakes up as the pallet hits the ground, with packets of food, soap, razors scattered around him. Peasants are coming out of the woods to gather up the supplies from the Red Cross drop, and they see him. Before he can figure out what is happening, gunfire breaks out and those interested people begin to fall to the ground, bleeding and dying. This gets his attention and he takes cover, then begins to run. In his flight he sees a dead elk, as well as soldiers' bodies. He finds a road and flags down a U.N. truck, shouting that he's English.

The truck doesn't want to take him, but a BBC newsman onboard takes pity on him and they haul him into the truck and slap a helmet and flak vest on him. The next thing he knows, they have pulled into an emergency hospital camp. And the BBC guy is filming. The punk kid goes inside just as they are about to saw a man's leg off without anesthetic. The guy is screaming. The kid is shocked by this, but the BBC man explains that they have no drugs left and if they don't take the leg, he'll die.

The boy tells the doctor to wait—just *wait* a minute. And out of his pocket he pulls his stash of heroin. Spoon, lighter, syringe. He quickly melts the narcotic and loads the needle. Then he shoots up the patient, whose screaming subsides. A look of peace and a smile spread across his face as the heroin gives him relief, and he is holding the kid's hand as the doctor takes his leg.

This is an amazing, completely unexpected turn of events. In five minutes of film this kid, a complete loser, doomed to die a pointless waste of a death, is transformed into a humanitarian hero. It's an amazing sequence, one of those pieces of film that make us remember we can do anything. A movie can take us anywhere. This is the real magic.

Then Jasmin Dizdar, the filmmaker, tops it. While this amazing thing is happening in Bosnia, at home in his London suburban house, his mother is cleaning his room and is shocked to find drug paraphernalia under her son's bed. She shows it to her husband and they are, of course, horrified. When the kid finally comes home, stumbling into the house, having been airlifted out with the BBC, he is so exhausted, his parents' fury doesn't even register. But as they rant and rail, behind him on the television are images of the war and the young hero who managed to smuggle in much-needed drugs that no one else had been able to supply. And of course, it is their boy. Their jaws drop; they are struck dumb in disbelief.

Are we having fun *now?*

This is what we aspire to: the unexpected, original turn of storyline or character. The surprises that keep screenwriting endlessly interesting.

CHAPTER 17

Dialogue

Writing great dialogue is a very specific art. Those who do it best are seldom out of work. If you study your favorite movies, you will begin to notice that the dialogue is much leaner and more succinct than the way people actually talk in everyday life. Learning to hone and trim ordinary language into film dialogue is a craft that requires you to develop the skill of a poet.

For me, *Good Will Hunting* was somewhat sophomoric, full of predictable psychology, but it had one great scene in a bar where the smart street kid tells off a cocky Joe College jock in the ultimate fabulous runs-circles-around-him speech that everyone wishes they could have delivered just once in real life. It never happens, of course. It is a speech that probably took three days to write and three minutes to deliver. We love it. And it won the boys (Matt Damon and Ben Affleck) an Oscar for their screenplay.

That year, *As Good As It Gets* was a far better piece of writing. It was surprising all the way through, with lines that were at the same time stunningly true emotionally and completely unexpected. We almost never get this in a movie. It took a new writer, Mark Andrus, outside the insulated Hollywood culture, to conceive the idea. He summarizes the concept as "a movie about the worst man in New York City." Who would've thought that would make a great movie? Surprise!

After Andrus wrote the original screenplay and sold it, it took a writer as brilliant as James L. Brooks to revise and polish it for a full year to get the final version. Something that beautifully crafted doesn't get tossed off in a couple of weeks. My favorite line is Melvin Udall (Nicholson) to a bartender: "And such a woman . . . if you make her laugh, you got a life." You know this is the truth for this guy, as economically phrased as a Japanese haiku.

Rules of Thumb for Writing Dialogue

☑ **When in doubt, cut it out**. Tighten your dialogue to as few words as necessary. I cut the words *just, really, so, very,* and *well* when it is a sentence opener, as in "Well, I think . . ." Also, when one character asks another a yes or no question, you can often cut the *yes* or *no* answer. For example:

> GUY: Do you want to go out Friday night?
> GIRL: No. I'm sorry.

It's often better if she just says, "I'm sorry." Or even merely, "Sorry." This is the direction you want to go when polishing your screenplays. Use as few words as possible.

☑ **Names**. Don't have characters call each other by name in dialogue, unless it's for a specific effect, such as a threat. Once is enough. None is okay, too. In real life, people rarely use each other's names when they are talking.

☑ **Less is more**. In great dialogue, the screenwriter gets to the heart of the matter in the fewest possible words. In a novel, a character can say, "I have three things I want to talk to you about, and the first one is the problem I'm having with Jane." In a movie you go straight to, "I'm having a problem with Jane." No beating around the bush. Keep it lean and cut it clean. Occasionally, screenwriters can get the dialogue so compact it can become poetry.

Ron Hutchinson wrote *Murderers Among Us: The Simon Wiesenthal Story* for HBO. In one scene, Simon (superbly played by Ben Kingsley) has been released from a Nazi death camp and sits emaciated and alone on a cot in a hospital ward. He assumes his wife has not survived the camp, but she appears in the doorway, equally emaciated, and slowly walks over to him. She is weeping as she puts her arms around him, and as she touches him he begins to cry as well. She asks, "Does it hurt?" And he answers: "Everything hurts." Two words. It is a powerful moment, made more so by compressing all of the emotion of separation, Auschwitz, and certain death, followed by resurrection and reunion—all of that into two words. *"Everything* hurts."

✅ **Three beats**. Make each piece of dialogue three sentences or less. The only exception might be a key speech, like a summation to the jury. If you need more than three beats, try breaking the speech up with a comment from another character or a piece of action. As you work with this, you'll start to see that nearly all lines can be boiled down to three beats, and they are almost always better for the cutting.

✅ **Don't hit the nail on the head**. In good dialogue, it's often more important to get the meaning right, but not come right out and say it in so many words.

In my script for *Buffalo Girls* (based on the novel by Larry McMurtry), when Calamity (Anjelica Huston) has to ride out to Blue's ranch and tell him that the love of his life, Dora, has died, she never says those words. She helps him mend a fence and Blue (Gabriel Byrne) senses something is wrong:

> BLUE
> Is Dora all right?

> CALAMITY
> She had a baby girl...this time
> the baby lived...

> BLUE
> The *baby* lived?

She nods. He gets it and his legs almost go out from under him.

Sometimes these moments have more impact if you convey the information by talking around it, by saying it indirectly.

Another example of this is an early scene in *Ordinary People*. It is after midnight. A father (Donald Sutherland) sees the light on under the door of his teenage son's room. He knocks and looks in. The kid has had a night-mare and is pretending to be reading, afraid to go back to sleep. This is the first dialogue we hear between them in the film:

> FATHER
> Trouble sleeping?
>
> SON
> No.
>
> FATHER
> Have you thought about calling
> that doctor?
>
> SON
> No.
>
> FATHER
> Well, the month is up. I think we
> should stick to the plan.
>
> SON
> The plan was *if* I needed to call him.
>
> FATHER
> Okay. Don't worry about it. Hey,
> I'm working on those Michigan State
> tickets.

The underlying tension in what they're not saying is electric. We are prac-tically leaning forward in our seats trying to figure out what is going on here. Something is clearly wrong. And what kind of doctor is optional?

What they don't say is, "It's been a month since you tried to kill yourself. I'm worried about you. Don't you think you should call that psychiatrist to make sure you don't get depressed and try again? I'm trying to be a good father, but I'm afraid I might push you over the edge so I have to tiptoe around very carefully." Get the idea? In the script, everything he's *not* say-ing is in there, all the emotion and the meaning—just not in so many words, which makes for better writing.

☑ **Give your characters individual voices**. Not every character in a screenplay should be equally smart or stupid, or from the same type of family, culture, education, part of the country, etc. Sometimes a screenwriter will try to make every line of dialogue a great line—and all the characters will start to sound like the writer on his best day. It doesn't seem real.

Shakespeare in Love won the Oscar for Best Picture. Screenwriters Tom Stoppard and Marc Norman managed to give each character an individual voice. All of the characters were from Elizabethan London, but some were aristocratic, some lowborn, some poetic, some sarcastic, like the acid-tongued Queen Elizabeth. Work hard to give each character his or her own voice.

☑ **Don't be afraid to try a completely original voice on occasion**. My favorite example of a wildly different voice in dialogue is Joel and Ethan Cohen's script for *Raising Arizona*. The small-time convict played by Nicolas Cage explains to the audience in the narration about his wife's infertility problem. The way he puts it is: "Her womb was a rocky place in which my seed could find no purchase." Pretty Biblical language for these trailer-park types, but the voice is consistent throughout and consistently hilarious. The character and voice mesh in an unexpectedly quirky and original way that absolutely works.

☑ **Read it aloud**. I used to get actor friends to come over and read a script to me. Failing that, I'd read the dialogue out loud to myself. Some lines that look fine to your eye won't fool your ear for a second. It shouldn't surprise us. Our ears have heard thousands of hours of movie dialogue, while our eyes have read far fewer screenplays. It's better to read it out loud and hear the rhythms now, than risk the embarrassment of sitting at the first "table read" with the stars and hear key lines clunk onto the floor like stones. Read it out loud, even if it feels silly. Just do it.

Let these examples encourage you to try some different approaches to writing dialogue. Remember, when in doubt, cut it out. Less is more. Limit each speech to three beats. Don't hit the nail on the head. Take some chances in your choice of vocabulary and make each voice unique. A great line of dialogue can be as clean and lean as poetry.

Take the following line, perhaps the most famous haiku ever written for the American Cinema. It's from *Casablanca*, screenplay by Julius & Philip Epstein and Howard Koch:

```
Of all the gin joints
In all the towns in the world,
She walks into mine.
```

CHAPTER 18

Heroes and Villains

et's talk about villains. Over the last 50 years, the Disney Animation group discovered that its most successful animated films were the ones with the best villains. You don't "get" *101 Dalmations, Sleeping Beauty,* or *Pinocchio* without Cruella DeVil, Maleficent, and Monstro. More recently, Jaffar and Scar provided the energy to propel *Aladdin* and *The Lion King* to monster-hit status.

For a story to work well, you must have a well-balanced adversarial struggle between worthy opponents. *Beowulf* would have been forgotten centuries ago, were it not for the monster Grendel.

In the last decade's action movies, we've been subjected to a group of vaguely European villains played by actors like Jeremy Irons, Alan Rickman, and Gary Oldman. They are smart but interchangeable, usually only motivated by large quantities of money. The problem is that they are two-dimensional and largely forgettable.

Then we've had a crop of ranting, over-the-top, maniac bad guys, played by actors like Dennis Hopper, Gary Busey, and John Malkovich. They are scary, loud, dramatic, and crazy. But also interchangeable. Think fast: Can you remember which villain was in which movie? The actors who play all of the above are unquestionably talented. It's the written characters that are lacking. So let's get to the heart of the problem: How to write a great villain.

A good antagonist needs to have strengths that equal the protagonist's, but don't necessarily mirror them. The adversary needs to be passionate about his own cause, no matter how evil or misguided it might seem to the audience. And he or she needs to be a real person (in whatever reality the movie is set). Let's use some recent examples of villains that have worked in movies.

1 **The man with a Mission**. In *The Peacemaker*, the villain is a man who has lost his wife and child in the war in Bosnia. He commits himself to a suicide mission to stop the madness of war and avenge his loved ones. He is not evil at all. He believes himself to be acting for God and for good, even though his plan includes detonating a nuclear device that will vaporize Manhattan. Our heroes (George Clooney and Nicole Kidman) are good at their jobs and want to save New York City, but the villain's passion and dedication transcend theirs. He cares more. This makes him a worthy opponent, even though they have all the technology and firepower of the U.S. arsenal at their fingertips.

2 **The match of equals**. In a movie like *Face/Off*, you get adversaries equally matched in intelligence, resources, and passion to kill each other. Nicolas Cage killed Travolta's son, and Travolta killed Cage's brother. They will kill each other or die trying. One is a straight-arrow lawman, the other as bad as they come. These elements alone will propel the movie engine on all cylinders. When they switch places, it gets even more fun.

It is a classic choice, this match of equals that fuels classics like *Gone With the Wind*. In case you didn't realize it, Rhett and Scarlett are very much adversaries. *Schindler's List* would have been half the movie without Ralph Fiennes's great counterpoint to Schindler. Add to these all the great westerns and gangster movies of the last hundred years, most of which have equally matched opponents.

3 **The match of equals who like each other**. *The Fugitive* is a flight-and-pursuit movie. Harrison Ford, on the run, and Tommy Lee Jones, in pursuit, are well-matched adversaries. And it works great that by the climax, Jones is eclipsed by the real bad guy and switches over to Ford's side. It also provides one of the few original touches to an action climax in a long time.

In *Heat*, the classic cop-and-robber drama by Michael Mann, he pits the greatest bank robber of our time (De Niro) against the smartest, toughest cop (Pacino). Halfway through they sit down for a cup of coffee together in a crackling, original scene. They discover that they know each other better than anyone else knows them and that they admire each other. Over coffee they come to like each other. The scene is played under the tension of the fact that they both know they will probably have to face each other in a gunfight and one will have to kill the other. The inevitability of this and the awareness of it only add to the suspense.

4 Devils and demons. When the bad guy is the devil himself and the hero is a mere human, the whole thing can get too far off balance. This is one of the reasons *The Devil's Advocate* didn't work very well. Even the smartest lawyer, played by Keanu Reeves, is no match for Pacino's Satan.

Fallen did work well. Its demon had to be in a human body in order to interact on earth. He was absolutely evil, but not omnipotent or invincible. A human being could take him on, and Denzel Washington was a worthy opponent. It was also a lot of fun having a disembodied demon that could instantly possess human beings, moving from one to another, by simple touch. It made a scary and original movie and gave the hero a whole new set of problems. For example, if the demon is in a body which is shooting at you and you fire back, you might kill an innocent schoolteacher—while the demon jumps into a passing child and gets away. Now you've killed an innocent person, been thrown off the police force, and are thought to be crazy, while the demon is gleeful at bringing you down. There is a lot of scriptwriting fun to be had here, and with no need to rely on special effects.

The Exorcist, the classic of this genre, worked in part because the priests were the best exorcists on earth and the demon was confined to a child's body. This constraint placed on the spiritual battlefield allowed the opponents a well-matched struggle in the war between good and evil.

5 Non-living adversaries. We don't have space to go into this one in detail, but these are the movies about comets, tornadoes, and hundred-foot waves, which are always big, scary, and dangerous. To balance this, you need to make your hero a world-class expert astronaut, tornado chaser, or swordboat captain. When you get a huge comet against just plain folks (the problem for *Deep Impact*) it's no contest—and the movie will suffer for it.

6 Monsters. We have a long and colorful history of monster movies—and some real stinkers, too. Why did *Godzilla* fail a few years ago? Well, for a lot of reasons, but let's boil it down to a simple formula: Godzilla vs. Matthew Broderick. Where would you put your money? Is that a fair fight between worthy adversaries? I love Matthew Broderick, but he's no match for a tyrannosaurus the size of the Chrysler Building.

One of our most successful monster villains in recent years was the mercurial menace of T-1000 in *Terminator II*, who was perfectly matched opposite the cyborg of superhuman Arnold Schwarzenegger. There was a lot of great entertainment to be mined there, and James Cameron came up with the gold.

7 Sub-human villains. Hannibal Lecter in *Silence of the Lambs* and *Hannibal* is certainly one of the most interesting of recent villains: an inhuman eater of human flesh. But even more than the remarkable performance of Anthony Hopkins, "the Hannibal effect" is created by all the right set-ups. These include the characters that surround Hannibal and treat him like the most dangerous object on earth, as well as all the lengths they go to to protect people from him—the hockey mask, strapping him to the stretcher, letting no one near him. All these details create the horror that is Hannibal. And they are all carefully written. Of equal interest is the adversarial relationship with FBI Agent Starling. In *Silence*, this worked well; with Jodie Foster's intelligence and Lecter locked up, they were well-matched opposites. His inhumanity is matched equally by her humanness, vulnerability, and dedication to saving lives. The light does battle with the darkness, each with their own opposite weapons. While neither is beaten, they walk away to engage another day.

Unfortunately, the balance between these two characters did not work as well in *Hannibal*. Why? With Julianne Moore's somewhat more feminine, not-quite-as-smart version of Agent Starling, and with Hannibal now at large, the balance was blown. Those are not well-matched adversaries. That Hannibal wins is no surprise at all. It was over before it began, and therefore less fun to watch. It's like a football game in which the less skillful side never gets within 20 points of the winning team.

8 Stacking the deck. My favorite hero's journey of recent years was *Gladiator*. Here is a story that would make Joseph Campbell happy. We meet the hero at the top of his form. He is the most glorified general of Rome, beloved by his troops, kicking butt in battle, chosen by Emperor Marcus Aurelius to succeed him. But by the end of the first act, he has lost everything: emperor and empire, family and freedom. What a journey he takes us on from that lowest point, through gladiator training, and triumph, to a final confrontation with the murderous Emperor Commodus, and a second chance to change the course of an empire.

The villain, Commodus, is a weak man and a coward. He manages to arrive just as the war ends. He has incestuous desire for his sister, who could supply him with "an heir of pure blood." And when his father tells him he has chosen Maximus to succeed him, he strangles the old man on the spot. He is a sniveling, slippery snake of a villain—arrogant, elegant, and scheming.

How do you make the story of *Gladiator* work when the hero, Maximus, is a Herculean warrior and the villain is a cowardly, incestuous whiner? Simple. You stack the deck. Give the wimpy Emperor Commodus all of the external power. He has armies, soldiers, the entire empire at his command. And strip the hero of everything but his hands, heart, and mind—then lock him up in chains and make him fight for his life every day. Through every step of the journey, Maximus is the underdog. And it works, absolutely. In a fair fight, it would have been over in ten seconds. So the storyteller has to stack the deck and rightly so.

9 The underdog-villain mistake. Spielberg, one of the godfathers of *Gladiator*, knew how to play the game of creating a great villain in *Jaws*, of course. Make the adversary the biggest, most insanely vicious shark in the history of the sea. But in *Hook*, he forgot what made the story of *Peter Pan* fun. His Pan (Robin Williams) was bigger than Captain Hook (Dustin Hoffman), and the lost boys were fully as big as and quite a bit tougher than the pirates. I'm sorry, but where is the fun in that? The fun of *Peter Pan* was about a few little boys beating a huge ugly bunch of pirates, including the biggest, meanest Captain of them all. We can learn from Spielberg's mistakes as well as his wins.

10 Villain as fallen hero. The absolute champion villain in movie history is undisputed. In terms of box-office grosses, he has outdone all contenders by hundreds of millions of dollars. I am referring, of course, to the ultimate villain, Darth Vader. When the first *Star Wars* movie screened, it got good exactly at the moment DV stepped onscreen with his gleaming black helmet, his eerie, mechanical breathing, and the melodious voice of the great James Earl Jones. Great trappings, to be sure.

But what made Darth Vader great was that he was a richly drawn character with story and motives and history and relationships. When we find out he is Luke's father, we don't say, *"WHAT?!"* because he already had a deep resonance for us. We *knew* he was somebody. All the pieces came together and made more and more sense. When he died in *Return of the Jedi*, we didn't ask, "Where's the next episode?" We knew that the saga died with him.

If you want your script to become a great movie, create a villain worthy of the name. Match him well to your hero and to your story, and you're set to make movie history.

CHAPTER 19

FADE IN: How to Write a Great Movie Opening

You've heard about the huge piles of scripts Hollywood producers and agents have to plow through. When they finally pick up yours, you've got about five pages to grab them or they'll move on to the next. How are you going to do it? Here are some pointers on how to write a dynamite opening for your script, using examples from movies you can rent at your local video store. (See Appendix A for a detailed list of movie openings to rent and study.)

Choose a strong image. The opening moments should convey your theme or set the mood for your film. In the opening credit sequence of *Norma Rae*, baby pictures of Norma growing up are intercut with images of the textile mill. As the endless spindles of thread are woven, the cycle of life is shown in a full circle, from Norma Rae's infancy, to Norma as a young woman holding a baby of her own. It gives us a feeling of hopelessness as we come to realize that not only will Norma Rae work in that mill, as her parents did, but her baby will probably grow up to work in that same lint-filled, unhealthy factory if something doesn't happen to break that thread. And that something, of course, is Norma herself, who stands up and defies the establishment. The entire theme and the heart of the movie are shown symbolically to the audience before the first word is even spoken.

In *The Mission*, we see natives in South America in the 1700s tie a missionary to a cross and push it out into the river, where a few moments later we see it plummet, like a crucifix, hundreds of feet down the face of a waterfall. The image is both breathtakingly beautiful and chillingly horrifying. It sets the tone perfectly for the clash of cultures that is about to unfold.

Introduce your star. It's a real asset to your script if your protagonist is introduced early. It's even better if his or her introduction is original and provides a clear revelation of character. The first scene in *As Good As It Gets* shows Jack Nicholson's character trying to coax a little dog onto the elevator before it pees on the floor. Failing this, he sends it down the garbage chute, with the words, "This is New York. If you can make it here, you can make it anywhere," as the little dog yips, echoing down floor after floor. We get it. This is the meanest guy in town, and it's funny.

Jump in with a bang. An amazing image, a mind-boggling enigma—these are great ways to start. The opening of *Close Encounters of the Third Kind* has jeeps arriving in a dust storm in the Mexican desert, where scientists examine an entire fleet of WWII planes that disappeared 50 years ago. The planes look brand-new. The engines turn right over. And the old man, with half his face sunburned, says in Spanish, "The sun came out last night and sang to me." We're hooked. What happened? What the hell is going on? These questions grab us, and we're off and running.

Symbolism. *Searching for Bobby Fischer* opens with a little boy, Josh, playing in a park with his friends. They are being knights with wooden swords. Then he stumbles on the high-speed hustle chess games in New York City's Washington Square. He finds a chess piece, a knight, and Laurence Fishburne appears, silently offering to trade him for a baseball. We don't know until the next scene which he picked, but the conflict of that choice—between being a regular kid and being a chess prodigy—is beautifully set up from the very first moments of the film. This opening scene also shows us it is Josh's birthday party (meaning that he is growing up and his life is about to change), and a storm blows in, which symbolizes change. If you study this five-minute sequence, you'll find it rife with symbolism.

Hit the right note. If it's a comedy, it had better be funny in the first five pages. *Pee-wee's Big Adventure* opens with a dream sequence of the Tour de France bicycle race. The French and Italian teams are streaking toward the finish line when they are overtaken by Pee-wee gleefully riding bolt upright on his 1950s-style Schwinn bike, wearing his gray suit and red bowtie. His character, his love affair with his bicycle, and the whole surreal Pee-wee world are given to us in one or two hilarious minutes.

Theme. *The Right Stuff* opens with black-and-white stock footage of planes in the 1940s attempting to break the sound barrier, while Levon Helm's voice-over tells us, "There is a demon that lives in the thin air behind a barrier called the sound barrier and any man who challenges him will die. Pilots came to the high desert of California. . . . They were called test pilots and no one knew their names. . . ." We are given the theme, told that this is going to be a true story about legendary heroes "pushing the edge of the envelope"—and that we are going to learn these heroes' names.

Establish relationships. *Butch Cassidy and The Sundance Kid* has a scene at the beginning where Sundance is accused of cheating at poker. Just as bullets are about to fly, Butch breezes in and tries to lighten things up. He barges right into the middle of the standoff, trying to talk the gunfighters out of bloodshed. Once the fight is averted, Sundance walks away and Butch gathers up his poker winnings. Within five minutes we get the whole story on these guys. They're married. Butch is the brains, planning the bank robberies and carrying the money, while Sundance handles the shooting. We know these guys by the way Goldman showed us, instead of telling us who they were.

What's the problem? *Face/Off* opens with an assassin (Nicolas Cage) trying to kill John Travolta as he rides a carousel with his small son. As he gets his sight set on Travolta's back and fires, the bullet goes through Travolta and kills the little boy. This event sets off the vendetta that lasts until the last frame of the film, with Travolta's character (not always played by Travolta) on an intense quest to bring his son's murderer to justice. And we are emotionally with him from the first moment of the film.

Surprise or astonish us. The opening scene in *Harold and Maude* is a classic. A young man comes into a room, lights candles, pins a suicide note to his lapel, and hangs himself. Then his mother comes in, unimpressed. Her response is, "I suppose you think that's very *funny*, Harold." And we're hooked. Of course he hasn't killed himself at all, but is just trying to get attention. And we are ready for a wild ride exploring the conversion of a young man from being infatuated with death to falling in love with life via the most surprising of love stories, between an 18-year-old boy and an 80-year-old Ruth Gordon.

In Appendix A I have given you a list of movies with great openings you can rent, along with a few notes on what to look for.

You too can write an original, dynamic, exciting opening sequence for your script. Rent these movies and watch carefully how deftly and simply the screenwriters and directors have done the job. Yes, there are big fish out there in Hollywood, but before you can land them, you've got to hook them.

CHAPTER 20

Act Two Blues

Good screenplays are solidly built in the classic three-act structure, as covered in Chapter Three. Which is the hardest act to pull off? That's right. The big, unwieldy Act Two. Second acts have been famous as the bane of playwrights for centuries. Now we screenwriters have inherited the problem. Here are some ways to help you heighten, tighten, and conquer those obtuse Act Twos.

Let's use the classic, and perfectly structured, film *Witness* as a model for how to solve Act Two problems. (Also easy to rent and review if you don't remember it well.) Act Two of *Witness* begins when the cop, John Book (played by Harrison Ford), arrives in Amish country to hide out and recover from a nearly fatal bullet wound, and it ends when the bad guys find out where he's hiding and come after him. How do the screenwriters (Earl W. Wallace and William Kelley) keep us interested for an hour-long second act of passive Amish non-action? Brilliantly. Witness the following:

1 Develop your B Story. This is often the love story. In *Witness*, Act Two is when the cop and the Amish woman get to know each other. She nurses him back to health. They dance to his car radio in the barn. They fall in love. You have time in Act Two to have two people believably fall in love.

2 Develop your theme. In *Witness*, the theme is the conflict between violence and non-violence—between the cop's urban culture and the idyllic Amish culture's pacifism and tranquility. This kind of pastoral world where people live in loving harmony with each other is something the cynical cop never thought possible. He might just as well have landed in Shangri-la. He has to deal with his own internal question: Can people really cooperate and live in peace? Book explores this idea by participating in a community barn-raising in the middle of Act Two. By having a direct, hands-on, physical experience of peaceful cooperation, Book gets a real, first-hand understanding that a harmonious way of life is possible.

3 Keep your A Story alive. Even though these themes and stories unfold quietly and are extremely low key, the second act of *Witness* works well, primarily because not 10 pages/minutes go by without revisiting the spine, or A Story—which in *Witness* is the story of the bad guys looking for Book, closing in on him, in order to kill him. This is done with phone calls from Book's partner, another cop (the only one he knows for sure is not one of the bad guys). His partner tells him things like: Stay out of sight. They know you're hiding in Amish country and they are searching for you. This underlying, building tension keeps the audience alert and interested through some pretty tranquil scenes.

4 Get your Set-Ups in place for Act Three. In the second act, John Book explains to the little Amish boy that guns are dangerous. He takes his apart and stores the bullets in a separate place. The gun itself is hidden in a big jar of dried beans on a kitchen shelf. Then, of course, when the bad guys arrive in Act Three, firing away with their own arsenal, Book can't get to his gun or bullets. And while the kid is trying to get them, Book has to fight the bad guys with no weapon, using other creative means. It's much scarier. Having the hero outnumbered is good. Having him outnumbered *and* unarmed as he is attacked by a bunch of guys firing away is better.

5 Continue to raise the stakes. Heighten the risks. Before the end of the second act, Book's partner is killed. This kind of event thrown into the second act helps to pump up the underlying tension. Having any escalating danger or imminent crisis playing under apparently passive, tranquil scenes will give those scenes bite and help them work.

Going beyond the example of *Witness*, here are a few other tricks to add to your bag that can help your second act keep ticking:

6 Shorten the time frame. Speed up the clock. Take a kidnapping story, for example. If the father has been given 24 hours to deliver $5 million, but the kidnapper begins to get nervous and suspects something is afoot, he could suddenly tell them to "have the money here in an hour or the kid's dead." Clearly, less time makes this story more interesting. A sudden jump on the clock can really help that old second act accelerate to a more exciting speed.

7 Roadblocks. The biggest reason that second acts sag is insufficient conflict. If things are dragging, throw stumbling blocks in your character's path. Get your characters into a situation where there seems to be no way out. In *Face/Off*, our hero, Archer, who has been surgically altered to look like the villain, is thrown into a maximum security prison. Then the only people (except for one) who know who he is are killed. And that one person who knows is not only the ultimate villain, but has Archer's face and identity and is living with Archer's wife and teenage daughter—and they both think he's Archer. It feels like there is absolutely no way out, and the tension soars. A good road block will do that for you. It can be anything that stops the progress of the ongoing story and forces the characters to find another way over or around a new problem.

8 Reversals. When things are rushing along in one direction, and they suddenly do a 180-degree switch and speed off in the opposite direction, that's a reversal. In a movie like *The Peacemaker*, Nicole Kidman and George Clooney think they've managed to delay the terrorist on his way to New York City with a nuclear bomb by holding everyone on the plane in customs. Then they find out that their man is a diplomat and has already been whisked through, bypassing customs. The terrorist is already loose in the city with the bomb—the exact opposite of what they (and we) believed to be the case. Reversals work best if they come out of left field, as the last thing your characters (and audience) expect.

9 Character revelation. Often in second acts, you have the luxury of time to explore your characters more deeply. You might choose to have the central character reveal a secret from his past. What makes him tick. In *L.A.*

Confidential, Bud White (Russell Crowe) is a wound-up, violent cop, used as the strong-arm by the corrupt police captain. Bud is also known for viciously pursuing wife beaters and rapists. In the second act he confides to his new lover, a glamorous hooker played by Kim Basinger, that when he was 12 his father tied him to a radiator and he watched his father beat his mother to death with a tire iron. It explains a lot about the man, and gives us new sympathy for what might have otherwise been an unsympathetically violent character. This kind of character work is often best played out in Act Two. In Act One we're too busy getting the ball rolling. And Act Three is for winding things up.

10 Develop your relationships. Now that your characters are in the middle of a story and basically stuck with each other, this is a good time to have them get to know each other at a deeper level and develop those relationships. Even in a film like *Gladiator*, in the second act the gladiators develop relationships and new loyalties with each other. These relationships go beyond friendship and camaraderie. By the end of the act, they depend on each other for their very survival. Relationships always work best in movies when they tie directly into the Through-line and support it. It is a great use for the time and space available in the second act.

With the right ingredients mixed and stirred carefully, your second act can be as dynamic and fast-moving as the other two. Don't be afraid to spice it up.

CHAPTER 21

Climaxes

The climax of the film comes near the end of Act Three. Sometimes it is the end of the film, but not always. I have separated Climaxes and Endings into two chapters, the difference here being that the Climax is about energy, all the waters rushing into a big, breaking wave. And the Ending is about wrapping it up. Tying up loose ends. This is a chance for the author to have the final word and make the point with a last perfect image or line.

The climax of the movie is the moment at which the Central Question is answered. Whether that question is, "Do the bad guys win?" or "Does the boy get the girl?" it must be answered in the climactic scene.

The tension must be broken. The energy that has held us throughout the film must be released.

As author Bill Johnson tells us, "A story is a promise." And at the climax it is time to deliver on that promise and pay off all those set-ups.

As you wrote the script, you probably had a pretty clear idea what that climactic scene would be. It was in the scene cards, fit into the proper slot on your storyboard. It may not turn out exactly as you planned it, but it will probably be pretty close.

As in all phases of the screenwriting process, you have a lot of choices here. Let's explore a few of them.

Obligatory climaxes. Sometimes the climax is dictated by the nature of the story itself. If you're doing *Rocky*, the big fight is the climax. The same is true for the final game of the series in sports movies. Or the meteor is deflected from destroying Earth at the last moment. When you promise the big bang, you deliver the big bang. Nothing less will do. Just watch out for the danger lurking in those obligatory endings: the lack of surprise.

The action genre climax trap. The action-adventure genre has gotten locked into obligatory endings with no surprises. It almost always has to end in either a shootout, or a bomb is defused or explodes. (For "bomb," substitute comet, volcano, tidal wave, etc.) That's about it. These two choices are slim pickings indeed. To swipe a cliche, they run the gamut only from A to B. It's gotten so bad that the only difference in climaxes in these movies is where they're set. The good guy shoots or punches it out with the bad guy on top of a speeding train (*Broken Arrow, Mission Impossible*), speeding boat (*Face/Off*), in a factory (*Terminator II*) or shipyard (*Eraser*), and so on. It's *Gunfight at the O.K. Corral*, just picking a different corral. When an action movie finds a new and different ending, we are delighted. But it almost never happens.

The Fugitive, while it still had the punching match atop a tall building, was fun because the two guys who had been pitted against each other throughout were suddenly both on the same side. It was a breath of fresh air.

How subplots can support the climax. Every subplot has its own three-act (or at least three-beat) structure and its own climax. When your subplots climax simultaneously with your A Story, it gives far more impact to that climax. It is like loading your cannons with that much extra explosive charge. Here's an example. At the climax of *Tootsie*, when Dustin Hoffman, on live TV, pulls off his wig to reveal that America's favorite soap opera diva is actually a guy, it gets a huge laugh. Now, the audience watching the movie *Tootsie* already knows Dustin Hoffman is a man, so why the big laugh?

Why? Because there are more than a dozen subplots to *Tootsie*. It was rumored at the time that more than a dozen writers were involved in the credits arbitration by the Writers Guild on the picture. And it seems like every writer added a subplot. A brief rundown:

Hoffman's career as an actor/actress.
His romance with Jessica Lange.
His girlfriend, Teri Garr.

JL's dad, Charles Durning, who wants to marry him.
The chauvinist soap star wooing Hoffman as well.
His best friend Bill Murray.
His ongoing battle with his agent.
The creator of the soap, for whom "Dorothy" is a savior.

Well, you get the idea. So when he pulls off the wig, it's the climax of *all* the subplots. And as we cut to the reaction shots (or shocks) of all of the above, the hilarity builds and builds. It worked great. In fact, it turned a silly idea into a pretty good movie. (I mean, if Dustin Hoffman in drag waited on you in a restaurant, would you for one second think he was a woman? Me neither.)

Offscreen climaxes. Occasionally the climax is offscreen. In *The Winslow Boy*, for example, the final verdict of the trial is not shown. We get the information told secondhand. It is somewhat weaker this way. In this case, it is a holdover from Terrence Rattigan's stage play, and David Mamet, as a man of the theater, chose to stay with that. We are deprived, as an audience, of the emotional high of that victory. We are given a much lower-key, less emotional version. I missed the moment.

In *Erin Brockovich*, we don't see the moment in which the final verdict is handed down, but I didn't miss it at all. Instead of showing the courtroom scene, Susannah Grant chose to take us back to the home of the first victim we met, to sit with her as Erin tells her that her family will get five million dollars. This is a far more personal, emotionally charged moment, and it pays off tremendously.

Surprise climaxes. These are rare but can be amazing. *Gladiator* did a total third-act 180 from where its set-ups were heading, and it gave the film a feeling of, "oh my god, everything is going wrong!"—which was great. In the third hour, it definitely got our attention and kept us right with it.

There were at least a dozen set-ups telling us the plan:

Maximus's freedom would be bought, backed by wealthy senators and Lucilla. He would be spirited out of the gladiator's prison, smuggled out of the city, guided by his faithful servant Cicero, to be reunited with his army camped nearby at Ostia. Then he would lead that army back into the city, where it would overthrow Commodus and restore Rome as a republic. Many scenes and much dialogue were spent to set this all up.

Then what happens?

Lucilla gives him the word: It's tonight.

The gladiators fight to give him cover to slip away.

He escapes from the jail.

He goes to the rendezvous, and it's a trap. Cicero is the bait and is killed.

Maximus is captured and much, much worse off than ever before.

This sets the stage for a whole *new* climax, one that we were not prepared for. And this very lack of emotional preparedness helps give the whole last section more raw emotional energy.

You might think, "Why did we need all those set-ups and planning if none of it came to pass?" Well, we have to be moving through the story with intention and direction. We need a plan and a goal—even if it's never reached. The movie is the journey, not the destination. And all that plotting and planning made a dynamic second act in a movie that was more than three hours long. Without the "conquer Rome" plan, they would have been in big second-act trouble.

One of the things we are always trying to find, as screenwriters, is "the darkest hour before the dawn." This moment has to come before the climax, and the darker and less predictable it is, the better.

CHAPTER 22

Writing a Great Ending

How important is the ending? Here's a little story, which some of you may know. Thomas Hardy was the most popular novelist of his day. He wrote many books, now classics, such as *Far From the Madding Crowd* and *Tess of the D'Urbervilles*. And like Dickens before him, he serialized them in periodicals. His readers were avid and loyal.

Then he wrote a novel called *Jude the Obscure*. It is a good book until the last section, in which something so outrageous, shocking, and gratuitous happens that it is unforgivable. The book was made into a film as well, starring Kate Winslet, of *Titanic* fame. The movie was also a failure. Actually, it was a good movie—up until that last ten minutes. As I watched the film, I was thinking, "This is *good*. I'd recommend this to my friends." Then *whammo*. What happened? Don't worry, I'm going to spoil it for you right now, since it's not worth rushing out to rent.

Jude is the story of a bright young man who is denied entrance to a university because he comes from the working class. He is a stonemason. He marries foolishly. When his wife deserts him, he falls in love with his cousin, who has also made an unloving, hasty marriage. They are soul mates (or the English equivalent, at any rate), and she leaves her husband for Jude.

They live as husband and wife, in love, having children, but no marriage certificate. Each time this is discovered, they get fired/evicted and have to move on to another town where they are not known. Then, just when things are looking up, they come home to find that Jude's sweet little boy of around seven has killed his two siblings (a toddler and an infant) and then hanged himself. *What?* Get the picture?

After the uproar over *Jude the Obscure*, Thomas Hardy lived another 25 years but never wrote another novel. Now there is a life sentence we can pity him for. We all know how painful not writing can be.

We need to be consciously aware of how we are ending our work. The final image is what the audience is left with. The ending will become "the author's message," whether we want it to or not. For once, we get the last word. We can use it to inspire, shock, amuse, or educate. We can make them cry, laugh, or think.

Let's explore some of the possibilities for endings:

The Big Win. As in: Rocky flattens Apollo Creed. James Bond/Batman/Bruce Willis saves the world from being destroyed. The football/basketball/baseball team wins by a hair in double overtime. Luke Skywalker blows the Death Star to smithereens. You know the ones. All of those are Big Win endings. The only thing tricky about making these work is playing against the inevitability of the victory. We have to think (even though we *know* they're gonna win) that they might not.

Union Endings. Boy gets Girl. The wedding at the end of the Jane Austen adaptation. The big kiss at the end of nearly every classic Hollywood love story ever made. These seem basic, but there are many movies that have great clinch endings and wouldn't be great any other way. It doesn't have to literally be a kiss, of course. Sometimes all he has to do is take her hand, as in *Sleepless in Seattle* or *South Pacific*. It can be a look, a line, a moment. There are an unlimited number of ways you can play this. It is almost always an audience pleaser, and often it's the best way to wrap it up.

You can combine endings. For example, *The African Queen* offers a Big Win and Boy gets Girl, both. They win for the Allies and they win each other. A double pay-off can be doubly satisfying.

Reunion Endings: Coming Home/Completion. Examples range from *The Killing Fields* to *Home Alone*, and many places in between. These can be some of the most powerful and emotional endings you can create. *The Killing Fields* is my favorite. *Sounder*, a children's classic, similarly ends with a great reunion scene, as the father, long missing, comes home again.

Buttons. A button is a small thing at the end of a movie (or at the end of a scene) that is a little surprise. It is a moment, word, or image that gives the movie a lift. *Kramer vs. Kramer* is a great example of an ending with a strong button. In the final scene, it comes after the Reversal. Having won the custody battle, the ex-wife, played by Meryl Streep, comes to pick up her son and take him away, but instead tells Dustin Hoffman, that she has changed her mind. She's not going to take him after all.

Streep says she wants to go up and talk to their little boy. Hoffman suggests she go up alone. As she steps into the elevator, she tries to dry her tears and smooth her hair. She asks him, "How do I look?" He says, "Terrific." And she looks surprised and he smiles—and the elevator doors slide shut. Great button. It works like a good button should, to give the audience that little surge of lift at the last moment. This one means hope, happiness, a glimmer of sunlight at the end of a stormy movie.

A button can accomplish an enormous amount in a split second. It can uplift an audience and have them leaving the theater in a different frame of mind. A great button might not make the difference between a hit and a flop, but it can make the difference between a moderate hit and a big hit. Watch audiences as they leave a movie theatre. Movies with great buttons have audiences walking out feeling like they just saw a great movie—which is how word-of-mouth happens.

Coming Full Circle. Coming back to where we began is an old and honored storytelling tradition. Sometimes it is the best choice and feels completely right. Don't force it, but if it comes to you naturally, embrace it.

I wrote a TV movie called *Best Friends for Life*, based on a novel by Shelby Hearon, which starred Gena Rowlands, Linda Lavin, and Richard Farnsworth. It came full circle in a clear, strong way that makes it a useful example.

FADE IN: In the opening scene, Sarah (Linda Lavin) walks with her dog in the woods. When she comes to a split in the path, she stops and waits for her dog to choose which way they'll go. He takes the left fork and she follows him. As he stops to sniff around, she decides he's chosen a good spot and she picks up a stick, digs a hole, and out of her pocket pulls an urn of her recently deceased husband's ashes, which she buries there.

The story unfolds over the course of the movie. She has a romance with the old country doctor Will, played by Richard Farnsworth. They get together when she says his dog looks just like hers, and they turn out to be from the same litter.

The last scene is (you guessed it) the two of them, Sarah and old doctor Will, out walking their dogs through the same woods. The dialogue goes like this:

                    SARAH
          We're so lucky.

                    WILL
          How do you mean?

                    SARAH
          That we happened to have pups
          from the same litter. That's
          how we got together.

                    WILL
          That wasn't luck.

                    SARAH
          What do you mean?

                    WILL
          I went out to Grady's farm and
          asked for one of those pups
          when I heard you had one.

                    SARAH
          You did? Why?

                    WILL
          In case someday I had the
          opportunity, I'd be able to say
          "Hey, we oughta get these dogs
          together sometime."

```
                           SARAH
                     (grins, pleased)
                Well, I stand corrected.
                     (takes his hand)
                I'm so lucky.

And they walk on together. When they come to the
place where the trail forks, this time the two dogs
lead them off to the right.

FADE OUT.
```

Sarah is back to the same place, only this time instead of losing a mate, she finds one. Full circle.

Coming full circle can be more simple, perhaps merely a mirrored image from the opening scene. *Working Girl* begins with a push-in shot on Manhattan as our smart, ambitious young heroine, Tess (Melanie Griffith) rides the Staten Island Ferry to work as a secretary on Wall Street. By the end she has fulfilled her dream of becoming one of those Suits in the executive suite with a secretary of her own, and the camera pulls back from that office window—in the exact reverse of the shot from the one at the beginning. Same shot, whole new world for our *Working Girl*.

Surprise Endings. If you love surprise endings and want to try one, study *The Usual Suspects*. It offers the most successful surprise ending in recent years. *The Sting* in its time also delivered a big, fun surprise. The Surprise Ending is not hard to do. It relies on a series of misleading Set-Ups. All the arrows point left, then you suddenly turn *right*. These are carefully designed in the Scene Card/Storyboard stage of the process.

Lost Treasure Endings. There is a long tradition in Hollywood of not letting the treasure seekers keep the loot, from the earliest silent versions of *Aladdin* onward. If you're interested in these, check out *Raiders of the Lost Ark*, in which the Biblical Ark of the Covenant, when it is finally dug out of an ancient tomb, is buried at the end in some gigantic government warehouse where it will never see the light of day again. The same is true in Indiana's *Last Crusade* where the Holy Grail is finally discovered—and immediately drops into a bottomless pit. Even in *Titanic*, which aims to please a crowd in every way, the egg-sized blue diamond is dropped into the deep blue sea. This is a time-tested tradition, but it's not a rule. If you want your characters to keep the treasure, go for it.

When the Bad Guys win. These are usually chilling and unsettling. Good examples of these include *Invasion of the Body Snatchers*, *The Omen*, *Arlington Road*, and *Fallen*. Up to the last moment, the audience thinks somehow the good guys will win. Then the final card is played, and it's bad news. When the button is right, these endings can work just as well as their opposites.

The End (Not Really). There are two types of these endings. One is the fake ending in the horror genre where we think the killer/monster/villain is dead, and then he grabs us one more time. Or the hand comes out of the grave to grab the girl in *Carrie*. Fun and legitimate, except when it becomes too predictable, as it has in this genre at the moment. In the other version, a story is left hanging deliberately in order to set up the sequel, as when Darth Vader gets away at the end of *Star Wars*—to return and fight another day.

The End, or Is It? This type usually works best when the "or is it?" is subtle. We think all the aliens have been destroyed, but as the relieved family walks through the vegetable market, the camera picks up an alien pod among the pumpkins. That kind of thing.

Unfinished Endings. It is perfectly fair to leave the audience hanging. Don't tell them what happens at the end. If they are engaged enough in the movie and come out arguing over what should happen after the final FADE OUT, fine. You have to get them and keep them in the movie for the whole two hours. "The Lady and the Tiger" is a short story that has become a classic for not telling the outcome. Likewise *Rashomon*, the Japanese classic film, has no resolution. The most recent example of this working hilariously well was Guy Ritchie's *Lock, Stock and Two Smoking Barrels*. Stopping just short of the punchline got a huge laugh.

Gratuitous Death Scenes. I've already talked about *Jude*, but unfortunately there are too many other examples of the "big D" being misused. These are the ones where you suspect they only killed off one of the main characters in the last few frames to make the audience cry. It's a cheap way to get an emotional response, killing someone off when the death doesn't fit the story or theme. There are many great movies that absolutely should have a central character die at the end, from *King Kong* to *Gladiator*. *American Beauty*, yes. The character's death *is* the point. What is life? We look at it from the perspective of being on the way out.

Gratuitous Death Scene endings, however, would include *Pay It Forward*. The way the child dies comes so out of left field that it makes no connection to anything that came before. What is the point? The good die young? Do a good deed and God will strike you dead? I think this original, well-intentioned movie would have done a lot better without the pointless crucifixion and the sappy, sad scenes that followed it. Meg Ryan hit by a truck at the end of *City of Angels* had almost a mean, bratty, *nyah-nyah-nyah* undertone to it.

Other ways to blow it. *Pearl Harbor* blew it in the last few seconds when the voice of the young nurse played by Kate Beckinsale under the final frames says, "After the Dolittle raid, the Japanese realized they couldn't win the war and began to pull out." Excuse me? This is such an enormous whopper it is hard to understand how they had the guts to tell it. What about the war in the Pacific and the thousands of men who died in it? And why on earth, if that were the case, would we drop *two* atomic bombs on Japanese cities? It's this kind of idiocy that gives Hollywood a bad name.

Baffling Endings. Sometimes an ending that has people debating what really happened long after the movie has ended can be a great boon to the movie. *Memento* has a website devoted to this discussion, and much of its success has been from people seeing it several times, trying to figure it out.

Shocking Endings. The ending of *Gallipoli* was stunning because the set-up was based on our expectation that things always turn out right in movies. The handsome young hero (Mel Gibson) is racing to save the day. In movies, he always arrives in the nick of time. But in *Gallipoli*, he arrives seconds too late and the result is hundreds of boys being slaughtered pointlessly right before our eyes, shocking us into the realization that this is not just a movie. This event really happened. Those boys were real and they *were* pointlessly slaughtered, and we feel the shocking impact of that.

Joke Endings. The greatest example of this is *Some Like It Hot* ("Nobody's perfect.") *The Front Page* also had a fun punchline with, "That sonofabitch stole my watch." There has been a fad of tricking people into sitting through the credits by occasionally delivering one more joke or outtake after the credits have rolled. It may have started with *Ferris Bueller* coming back on screen from the shower to admonish the audience with, "What are you still doing here? It's over. Go home." Jackie Chan has a tradition of showing funny mistakes and outtakes from his movies during the final credits. If you're writing comedy, keep the end-credit options in mind.

Practice Fixing Endings

You can learn a lot from movies that almost work or that work pretty well. (As opposed to movies that are awful. It's difficult to learn much from a movie that does everything wrong.)

Try this exercise on your own: If a movie had you nearly all the way through and then lost you right at the end, fix it yourself. Rewrite the ending, even if only mentally.

Ask yourself, "Why didn't it work for me? What about it was emotionally unsatisfying? What did I expect? What was I promised by the story that it didn't deliver? What Set-Ups didn't pay off? What about the Pay-Off was poorly set up?

It may be easier to get a feel for this with a specific example. How about *You've Got Mail*? A monster hit which most of you will have seen, it's close to perfect.

The movie is fresh and funny (though it is a remake of an old favorite, *The Shop Around the Corner*, an Ernst Lubitsch confection from 1940, starring James Stewart and Margaret Sullavan). Like its predecessor, *Mail* has charm galore and chemistry to spare between the delightful Tom Hanks and the adorable Meg Ryan. So why does the ending feel like a let-down?

The premise is this: Meg Ryan, owner of a sweet little independent shop for children's books, has a romantic e-mail correspondence with a man she is falling in love with unseen, online. What she doesn't know is that her pen pal is here arch-rival, the hated Joe Fox (Tom Hanks) of the Fox mega-bookstore, who is putting her shop out of business.

Halfway through the movie, Hanks finds out that his love letters are from her, but she doesn't find out until the end.

Here is the Final Scene—as filmed:

Cathleen (Meg Ryan) is walking with Joe (Tom Hanks) on the streets of New York. Joe asks her if they hadn't been enemies, does she think they might have had a chance of being happy together. She ducks the question, but is clearly thinking about it. She says she has to go—and breaks away from their conversation. She has a blind date to meet her anonymous penpal.

She goes to the park to meet the unknown man. When Joe shows up with his dog, Brinkley (whom he's written her about) she realizes he *is* Mr. X. She begins to cry and says, "I hoped it would be you." And they kiss. And we smile, and it's sweet. And we're happy, and somebody begins singing "Somewhere Over the Rainbow." But we feel—I don't know—not *great* about this. Why?

Because she didn't *choose* him. She ended up with him by default. It turned out there was no choice. A and B were the same guy. She's crying and we're not completely sure why. And neither is Joe, really. And she'd say the exact same words whether she really hoped it was him or not. So we don't know for sure.

Try this one on: CW's Version:

Cathleen and Joe are walking down the street. Same scene exactly. He says, "Don't go." She says, "I have to at least meet him. I can't leave him standing there." She goes to the park, waiting, more and more nervously, until she finally realizes (and says), "This is nuts. What am I doing?" And she runs off across the park heading for Joe's place and she runs into him coming her way. She bursts out with (perhaps with tears) talking a mile a minute. "I don't care who he is or if I never meet him. I love *you*."

And before she can say another word they are kissing each other, until a dog jumps up on them, interrupting them. When he says, "Down, Brinkley," she gets it and shrieks, "It's you! Why didn't you tell me!" And they're kissing again, and we pull back and the credits and old songs roll. And we walk out of the theater feeling great, as we should at the end of a romantic comedy.

Is this ending better? Yes. Not because I'm a better writer than the Ephron sisters. It's better because an active protagonist is better than a passive one. And a character making a choice is better than not making one.

Let's try to fix another movie with a different problem ending. Not to pick on Tom Hanks, but *Castaway* had a disappointing ending for a hit movie. The right ending seems so obvious that it is hard to figure out why they didn't film it. Were they trying so hard to be original or sophisticated or un-sentimental that they let their minds mess up the ending the heart intended? Watch out for this. For god's sake, let your heart write the ending.

In *Castaway* the hero, hapless FedEx employee Tom Hanks, is stranded on a desert island for four years. He has used the contents of the FedEx packages that have washed up after the plane wreck to survive. All except one, with angel's wings drawn on the box. That one has made it all the way home with him, unopened.

When he returns to civilization in Act Three, his old love has married someone else and has a baby. So, no happy ending there. He is feeling understandably alone and estranged from the world he once knew. So far, great. This is true and absolutely right. (I'm not saying we want sugarcoated fake finishes. Above all, audiences want to believe.)

Here's what happens next:

He carries that last package up to the house on the address (a house in which, as we have already seen, a beautiful woman artist lives, whose husband has been unfaithful and who is therefore available). And he knocks on the door and no one is home. So he leaves the package and drives away. On the highway, he chances to encounter that same lady. They have a brief exchange. Neither knows who the other is. Then she drives away.

He looks at the crossroads, tries to decide which way to go. Then, he gets a lightbulb-over-the-head expression of enlightenment—and turns in the direction the woman drove off in.

And that's it. We are left to assume that he went after her, they met, fell in love, and lived happily after, I presume. Or that at least there is the potential for that. A tiny glimmer of hope.

What's wrong with this? It is incredibly off balance with what *we* went through to get there. As an audience, we paid our dues bigtime, and we didn't get paid back. We suffered through four years of bleeding, starving, struggling, near suicidal depression, incredible loneliness and hardship, and then we suffered through losing true love. In emotional terms, we paid about $5,000 for this ticket, and got $10 worth of emotional payback. We were ripped off.

We not only don't get to see what's in the box, we don't even get to see it delivered to the addressee! Did you come out feeling disappointed? I was more than that; I was annoyed.

Here is what should have happened—in my opinion. And I'll bet you that same $10 that this was how it was originally written:

Tom Hanks, after having survived four years on that island, has been rescued, but lost Helen Hunt, and so on. He walks up to that farmhouse front door and knocks. The beautiful woman artist opens the door and says, "Yes?"

Tom says, "I have a delivery for you. It's a little late."

She takes the box and sees the date. She looks at him and recognizes him. Then she says, "Oh, my God. Thank you. Would you like a cup of coffee?"

He says, "It's not really our policy, but yes. I *would* like a cup of coffee." He goes in and the door closes. FADE OUT.

Is that too sentimental? I don't think so. I think it is what was promised. And a good movie delivers—even if the package is not always the one we expected. Great endings must be the emotional completion of the movies that have gone before them. The promise made must be fulfilled in some fashion, whether it is kept faithfully as promised or altered.

The best endings feel inevitable, whether they are happy, tragic, or hilarious. In your movie, you make the rules. The least you owe an audience is to play by them. And play fair. There are not many times in life when a screenwriter is given the last word. Use it wisely.

PART THREE

The Mind

Now is the time to take the whole, completed draft that the heart wrote, and shift back to the Left Brain to polish it up and bring some order to the chaos, without losing the life force. This is not about breaking it, but about cleaning it up, trimming the wild mane, strengthening the roar, maybe losing the whimper. Polishing, trimming, revising.

The Left Brain knows how to do this, but it's hard work that must be done. Take care that in bringing it to professional standards you don't kill the beast. The Left Brain must respect and treasure the work that has gone before. All four parts need to support each other.

To use another metaphor, it is an assembly line. The designer, welder, mechanic, and painter all need to work together, not tear each other's work apart. So polish it up now. Make it lean and clean. This is also the time to replace a cliché thrown in wildly with a better turn of phrase, a smarter way to express something.

The mind's work.

CHAPTER 23

Leaner and Cleaner: Polishing Your Script

In show business there is a saying, "Writing is rewriting." It is certainly at least half the story.

You've struggled and sweated and have a stack of pages that you are proud (and/or relieved) to have finished. Now you want the rewards: to send it out, sell it, get the praise and pay you deserve. Not yet. No agent or producer is looking for a first draft. They are looking for polished, lean, clean professional writing.

Where do you start? Take a cleanly printed copy and write on the first page "Working Draft." This breaks the ice and gives your mind permission to scribble freely on this copy.

I can't rewrite directly on the computer because I can't tell what I've done or if I've changed anything. I have to see the scribbling and notes to feel like I've accomplished anything. At first you may be discouraged seeing how much you change, but I have come to love the scribbled-on pages. I know the more I change, the better and crisper the finished work will be.

Being naturally lazy, I like to sneak up on this process. I start off planning to simply reread what I've written, but I have a pen in hand. The first time through, I trim excess words and things that aren't essential. If I come across a sentence that is awkward and a better phrasing occurs to me, I rewrite it. If a better way to say it isn't immediately clear, I write "AWK" or simply a big arrow in the margin and come back later. I keep a pad beside me so I can jot a list of other things I find and plan to change later.

When I've read through it once, quite a bit of ink will be splashed around. Next I look over the list I've made of things to fix. I always go for the easiest one on the list first and start with that. As you get warmed up and rolling the harder problems seem easier.

A Rewriting Checklist

Let's start with the numbers. Often you can figure out a lot about what's working or not simply from taking a script's measurements.

1 Check your act breaks. Are they in place? Does your First Act Turning Point come between pages 25 and 35? Does your Second Act T.P. come between pages 65 and 85? Do you get to the end within 5 pages after the Climax?

2 Measure the scenes. Are they all 5 pages or less? If one is longer, is this length merited?

3 Dialogue beats. Are all your speeches three beats or less? Can you trim and tighten those further?

4 The Domino Principle. Is every scene necessary? Page through and check to see if you have scenes that are expendable. If you cut one, does it change anything else? Usually scenes that can be lost without any damage to the rest of the movie will be lost in the cutting room anyhow. Might as well save time and money and cut them now.

5 Cut unnecessary words. If you don't need a word to express the thought, lose it. When in doubt, cut it out. My grandmother (a poet) used to say, "Why would anyone ever write 'at this time' when 'now' is a perfectly good word?"

6 Look for clichés and cut them. Find a fresher way to say "white as snow," "tall, dark, and handsome," etc.

7 Active verbs. Check to make sure you are using the active form of verbs instead of the passive. "Sarah stood at the window" is stronger than "Sarah was standing at the window."

8 There is not. Don't use "There is" to begin a sentence. "There is a man huddled in a black coat waiting for the bus." Better: "A man waits for the bus, huddled in a black coat."

9 The Lose 'Em List. I cut these words wherever I find them: "Just." "Really." "So." "Very." And usually "Well," when in dialogue: "Well, what shall we do?"

10 Names. In dialogue, don't have characters keep saying each other's names.

11 Cut unnecessary details. Give us enough to put us there. The sights and sounds. Too much detail just bogs us down. (Aha! Did you see that? I used 'just.' Wouldn't that sentence have been better "Too much detail bogs us down?")

I taught screenwriting at UCLA Film School for seven years and read hundreds of student scripts. I discovered there was one opening page that was most often used by new screenwriters: A slow pan around a bedroom as the protagonist (usually a college student) lies asleep in bed. At the end of the shot, which included every item on the floor, the desk, and walls, the reader was asleep as well. Tell us enough to let us see the room, don't tell us everything in it.

12 Read it aloud to yourself. Sometimes words that look good to your eye sound stilted to your ear. Reading aloud gets your brain to process the words in a different way.

13 Get feedback. If you are still having trouble getting a fresh perspective, you might ask someone to read it whose opinion you respect. But when you get the notes, use only the ones with which you agree. If a note brings up the feeling, "Of course, that's better," make those changes. If it makes you think, "I don't get it" or "I don't agree," then *don't* make those changes. You have to trust yourself first and last.

14 Have a Reading. It can be tremendously helpful to get six or eight friends to read the whole script out loud. It's actually better if they are not professional actors. A good actor can sell a mediocre line, and you're trying to find out which lines aren't great so you can fix them. So any old readers will do. A good line should work, even if your ten-year-old kid reads it.

Now let's tackle a big second draft issue: disguising that dull and boring exposition.

CHAPTER 24

Disguising Exposition

One way producers and agents determine the skill of a screenwriter is by how well the writer lays in the expositional information. Spend some time learning to camouflage the background information artfully, and you can master one of screenwriting's biggest pitfalls: exposition.

In the old days, stage plays used to open with the curtain rising on a drawing-room set. A maid would come onstage to answer a ringing phone: "Hello? Baron Richfield's country house. No, the Baron, Baroness, and their two children, Buffy and Muffy, have been in Paris showing their prize pugs and aren't expected to return until this afternoon." You got all the necessary information in the first 30 seconds. Except, of course, it was painfully bald exposition and bad writing.

The film equivalent is equally clunky. As a car speeds around a winding road, or we close on the cluttered office of a private detective, we hear his voice-over narration: "I'd been out of prison six months, off the booze for three, and in the private-eye business for a week when the Texas oil heiress walked in my door." Almost as bad.

How can we disguise our exposition so that it's not so dry and deadly? Here are some tricks for covering the necessary, but often dull exposition.

Show, don't tell. Instead of having someone say, "That Jesse James is a terrific rider and a dead shot," have Jesse come barreling in on a horse and shoot the cork off a guy's bottle in the cantina across the plaza, 50 yards away.

If you are writing *Flashdance*, don't have the girl meet a guy and when asked what she does, say, "I'm a welder but I also dance." No. Instead, you show a guy welding on a big construction job, huge helmet obscuring his face, sparks flying. Then when he lifts his mask, hey!—it's a girl! And when she goes home and drops the coveralls and puts on the music, she can *dance*. Showing, not telling, is what movies are about.

Don't tell me. I already know! Never have two characters say things to each other that they both already know just so the viewer can get the facts (unless they have some reason to repeat the obvious). Two brothers wouldn't say to each other, "You've resented me for ten years, ever since Dad turned his company over to me." However, there are exceptions, such as when you use the following:

Emotional camouflage. You can cover exposition with emotion. If these brothers were angry and yelling at each other, they could say that kind of thing. When fighting, people often say things they both already know. The emotion of the moment makes it possible: "You arrogant son of a bitch! You think his giving you the company means you can handle it?" Similarly, if someone is upset, crying, they can say things both already know and it can play naturally. "I was married to him for ten years and we only had sex when the surf report was lousy!" As a line of dialogue, this is lame. But if she's sobbing, it works much better. Laughing (whether induced by drinking, drugs, or exhaustion) can also cover characters repeating things they already know for our benefit. ("Remember that night in Nam/Paris/ Sigma Chi?")

Action! One of the best ways to cover exposition is with action. If you're flying an X-Wing at supersonic speeds down a narrow corridor of the Death Star, you can talk about being a kid "shooting womp-rats back home." The duller the exposition, the more interesting the action has to be to cover it. If the exposition is deadly dull, the character should be yelling it while running to a helicopter with bullets kicking up the dust at his feet.

Make 'em laugh. You can cover factual information with humor. In *Grosse Pointe Blank*, when someone asks John Cusack's character at his ten-year high school reunion what he's been doing since high school, he answers, "I went in the army, got recruited to be an assassin by the CIA, and now I'm a freelance professional killer." They laugh and think he's hilarious, but the audience got filled in on the back story. We all wanted to know how he got to be a killer.

In *Dirty Dancing*, some of the lamest background information is delivered by a young cousin while he and the girl are juggling watermelons, trying to carry too many. We are entertained by the melons, while our brains are getting the boring background.

Surprise! Have the information be unexpected. We expect that the Hispanic man the border patrol pulls out of the Rio Grande is an illegal alien. But when we learn that he's a blackjack dealer who ripped off a casino and is trying to escape into Mexico, we'll listen to the backstory with a heightened interest—because it's not what we expected. Surprises aren't that hard to do. They just require a misleading set-up.

Defuse a bomb. Play expository information against underlying tension. If a man is defusing a bomb, he can tell the young soldier beside him why his wife left him and we'll be riveted. (Hell, he could recite the phone book.)

Create an atmosphere of tension. This is all smoke and mirrors. Whatever the setting, you can usually find a way to add suspense and energy. In a scene in *All the President's Men*, Dustin Hoffman as a *Washington Post* reporter is in the living room of a reluctant witness getting vital, but dull, information about the Watergate scandal. She is giving him coffee, and the more he drinks, the more jittery he gets. And he is trying to remember everything she is saying without writing it down. He has to keep running to the bathroom and scribbling notes on toilet paper and stuffing it in his pockets. He is a newspaper reporter interviewing a key source and he doesn't even have a scrap of paper to write on? How likely is that? But it creates a wonderful anxiety as his pen keeps tearing the thin strips of tissue. It's funny as his pockets fill with wads, and it even gives us comedy and tension later as he tries to reconstruct his notes and read them to his partner. The information she gives may be key but fairly dull, but as he repeats it, we are still interested. How does this work? It's the old coffee-and-toilet-paper trick.

Make 'em late. If people are rushing and racing to get somewhere or even entering in a rush, apologizing for being late, it helps build enough energy to cover dull information.

What are they doing? Often exposition comes early in a script, where it may be too soon to cover with a major action sequence. You can use more ordinary action to cover. *The Contender* is a political drama, which is, by definition, a talking-heads movie. It includes scenes of jogging, golf, tennis, bowling, and basketball, in which the characters participate as they talk. Using so many different sporting events in a non-sports movie may be a bit much, but they keep the movie's blood pumping and that's the point.

Ask yourself what the characters might be doing as they exchange the necessary information. Steer away from restaurant scenes, meals in the dining room, breakfast at the kitchen table, talking while driving in cars, and phone calls. These are overdone, and visually static.

Take your cue from who the characters are. If it's a dad worried about a son, you could show him in the driveway, fixing the kid's bicycle. If it's a senator, he could be briefed by an aide while rushing into the underground tunnels to take the private subway tram to the basement of the Capitol Building.

If you put your mind to it, you can find interesting, original ways to fill the audience in on the necessary information as the story is rolling, so they are completely unaware that they've been briefed.

CHAPTER 25

Collaboration

Ben Hecht and Charles MacArthur, Ruth Gordon and Garsin Kanin, Matt Damon and Ben Affleck, Joel and Ethan Coen. There has been no shortage of great writing teams throughout the history of American film. If you have the kind of relationship with another writer that makes magic whenever you talk, that sparks each of you to greater and greater brilliance—and on top of that you have a personal relationship that can weather years of ego battles and petty annoyances and still be going stronger and longer than the best marriage you know—then God bless you. Go forth and collaborate. This chapter may be useful for you to read, but it is really intended for the other 99.9 percent of us who experience real problems with collaborating. At its worst, collaboration is twice the work for half the pay.

Once word gets out that you are a screenwriter, sooner or later someone will approach you with an offer to collaborate. It may be a close non-writer friend with a great idea. It may be a writer who thinks his or her project would be better written by the two of you. It may be a complete stranger who got your phone number from someone you once met, who wants you to help him tell (and sell) his grandfather's amazing untold story. Or it might be a director or producer who has an idea and a deal and wants to "write it with you"—usually meaning you write it, he criticizes it and takes half the credit and half the money.

There are hundreds of variations on these. My usual response is to thank the person and let them know that if I run out of ideas, I'll call them. Occasionally there are legitimate reasons for collaboration. But there are some drawbacks you should be aware of as well. First, let's clarify an intriguing issue surrounding the use of the conjunctions "and" or "&."

And and &. You've seen movie credits that say "Written by John Doe & Jane Doe and Bernie Smith." Why do they do this? Well, the "&" means that John and Jane are a writing team and work together, and in terms of residuals, bonuses, etc., are paid as a unit. "And" means that Bernie either rewrote them or they rewrote him. Chances are John & Jane never even met Bernie. This is why you sometimes get people accepting Oscars together who don't even look at each other or acknowledge each other. They may be complete strangers who resent having to share the limelight with someone who messed up their beloved script.

To do the math here, if this movie makes $100,000 in residuals over the next few years, Bernie will get $50K and John and Jane will get $25,000 each.

Drawbacks of Collaboration

Let's start with the down side. First, the biggest drawback is that if you write a script with someone else you only get half as much money. Studios don't pay twice as much for one script just because two people wrote it. So you need to consider carefully whether the work will be sufficiently better and faster with Joe to justify splitting the money with him.

Second drawback: One of the most important uses of a spec script, as I've said, is as a writing sample. It is proof that you can write, so that studios will hire you to develop other scripts for them. Now, if you submit a spec script with a partner, and you plan on being part of a writing team with this partner for the rest of your career, fine. But if you don't have those long-term intentions, remember that a script you write in collaboration on spec is almost useless as a sample of your individual writing. If someone is considering hiring you (alone) for a job, they want to see a script that you wrote alone. How do they know that the other guy didn't do all the work?

The third and probably most important drawback to collaboration is compromise. You won't have a real voice of your own. The way most collaborations work, nothing goes into the final script unless both writers approve it. That means you may come up with a detail or a line or a moment that you think is truly inspired, but if your partner doesn't like it, it's out. There is some danger of watering things down. Or of the result being that too many cooks spoil the broth and produce a less-than-great piece of work.

Advantages of Collaboration

There are indeed a few advantages, so let's take a look at the pluses.

When I was fresh out of film school and learning to write, I collaborated on screenplays with three different writing partners. After years of class deadlines, being out of school gave me more freedom than I wanted. So my major incentive in collaboration was discipline. I knew that my partner was going to show up at my house every weekday morning at ten o'clock and that we'd write till about two. It was an enforced routine that I hadn't yet developed on my own.

I also learned a great deal from my collaborators and vice versa. None of us ever thought we were going to be lifelong career teams, so there were no hard feelings when we moved on. One of them went on to a career writing and producing sitcoms, the second became a playwright, and the last now teaches third grade. I learned a lot. From the first I learned about writing comedy and comic pacing. The playwright taught me complex plotting. And the last showed me how to choose the right, unexpected details and to slow down and think things through more deeply.

None of the scripts we wrote together sold. It was only when I got confident of my own voice (after ten unsold spec scripts) that I finally broke in and started to get work as a screenwriter.

Consider the Credits

In a collaboration, the first thing that must be squared away before a single word is written is the issue of credits. Whose name goes first? If you wait until the script is finished to decide on this issue, it can turn into an ugly argument over who contributed the most, becoming a bigger problem than it needs to.

The matter can be decided by any number of criteria. It can be alphabetically—or by which sounds better. Butch and Sundance sounds better than Sundance and Butch, for example. And two a's don't work well together. Baretta and Brooks is harder to say than Brooks and Baretta. Try it out loud both ways and see how it sounds. Sometimes top billing goes to the person who came up with the idea for the project. Or to the person who is already established in Hollywood. Or to the one who does the typing.

Figure out what works for you and then stick to it. Teams become known with their names in a certain order. Lawrence and Lee. Rodgers and Hammerstein. Lennon and McCartney. Gilbert and Sullivan. Reverse the names and we don't instantly recognize the teams.

When friends or the press ask you who wrote which parts, do not answer the question. Present yourselves to the world as a team, equal in every way.

Collaborators' Agents

If you are involved in a long-term collaboration, it is essential that you have one agent and only one agent to represent the team. A writing team functions as a single writer; trying to juggle two agents, each representing one of you, would be impossible. If you both have agents already, you need to decide which one would best serve the team.

The Process

There may be as many variations on the collaborative process as there are writing teams. There are those teams in which one partner is the great talker, the idea person who paces and rambles on while the other takes notes, types them up into scenes, and does the painstaking work of getting it down and into script form.

Jim Cash and Jack Epps, Jr., the successful team that wrote *Top Gun*, as well as many other hits, lived in separate cities and never even saw each other. They sent drafts back and forth, taking turns editing and polishing.

Other teams hammer scenes out together; not one line is written down until both partners agree on every word. This style of collaboration makes for a uniform style and smooth dramatic build, though sometimes it involves verbal battling and occasional long stretches when it seems that a scene will never be finished.

Much of the comedy writing for screen and television is done by writing teams. It's like the old conundrum of wondering if "a tree falling in the woods really makes a sound." How can you be sure something is funny if there's no one else to laugh? The act of bouncing a comic scene back and forth, letting yourselves get sillier and more outrageous, often results in a much funnier scene. Go ahead and let it get totally ridiculous; you can always pull it back toward the center later. Some of the funniest moments in movies were created by two exhausted, punchy people in a burst of lunatic collaboration.

So if you write comedy, need discipline, or just go nuts locked in a room alone with the hum of your computer, find a good partner. The rest of us will enjoy having sole power over the first draft—and keeping the whole paycheck after the last.

CHAPTER 26

Writing and Rights

The best way (and practically the only way) to break into the screen-writing profession is by writing an original screenplay. Original means not based on anything else. There are no underlying rights.

A question that often comes up from writers is whether they can write a script about their friend/bank teller/mom's cousin. I'm not a lawyer, so this is not legal advice, but having a lot of experience as a writer of "docudramas," I strongly recommend not writing someone else's story if you don't have the rights.

There are, of course, exceptions:

Fame. If he/she is a celebrity, his/her life is considered to be in the public domain. But this doesn't mean just anyone who's been on the TV news or in the newspaper. This means really famous. If you asked ten people on the street at random, ten out of ten would likely know this person. O.J., yes. Marilyn, the Kennedys, Ted Kazinski, fine. But not the guy in your town who made the front page of your local paper for donating a kidney, or something on that level. It is generally assumed that most people with commonly known household names chose to give themselves to the public, either as celebrities or criminals, and therefore have given up their right to privacy by some level of choice. Unauthorized biographies (books, tabloids, or films) are part of the American culture.

Jackie Kennedy Onassis tried to block the TV movies about her; she was unsuccessful, even with the best lawyers money could buy. Grace Kelly only gave us permission to do her story after she read my script. But we didn't have it when I wrote it. A rare exception to this rule was Elizabeth Taylor.

Because she now owns a perfume business, her livelihood depends on her untarnished, glamorous image, so the court found in her favor; she was able to successfully block a network from doing a biopic on her. So aside from Liz or other cases of that nature, celebrities tend to be fair game.

Time. If the story you want to dramatize happened so long ago that no one involved is still alive, it may fall into the category of history and be public-domain material. We didn't have to get anyone's rights to depict characters in *Buffalo Girls*, for example, even though most of them were real people (Calamity Jane, Wild Bill Hickok, Buffalo Bill, etc.) and even though some of the real people, like Dora and Blue, were not famous.

You were there. If you were part of the story or present while it unfolded, you have the right to tell your version from your point of view. You don't have to get everyone else's rights, but always be careful not to libel anyone.

Get their rights. This doesn't always have to be expensive. It can be as simple as a letter wherein they give you permission to dramatize their story, and if it sells, they will be compensated fairly, the figure to be negotiated later. If you can't get the rights from the principal people involved in the story, you might try for one of the peripheral characters. (For example, if you can't get the septuplets' parents' permission, what about the grandparents, babysitter, best friend, etc.?)

Change the story. If you like the basic story elements but don't want to (or can't manage to) get the rights, you can tell the same basic story set in a different location with different characters—if you change basically everything. You can't do a fictional story about a female soldier taken captive during Desert Storm, because there were only a couple of them and they might each be able to make a case that you are doing *her* story.

I once did a TV movie called *Not in Front of the Children* starring Linda Gray and John Lithgow. It was inspired by a real case of a woman who lost custody of her children because she was living with a man without being married to him. We tried to get the rights to that real case, but the people asked for sums of money that were completely out of the TV movie ballpark. They wouldn't come down, so eventually we did a story set in another state where the laws were similar and changed their careers, ages, number and sexes of children, etc. We told the story as fiction, something that could happen rather than something that had.

Another example was a TV movie I wrote called *Jane Doe* which starred Karen Valentine, William Devane, and Eva Marie Saint. I got the idea from a newspaper story about a woman who was found naked, alive, buried in a shallow grave who had no idea who she was or what had happened to her. The problem was that, at the time, the mystery was still unsolved. I don't know if it ever was solved. So I just used the premise, changed the location, and everything else (killer, family, police characters, psychiatrist, etc.), and it worked out well. It was even nominated for an Edgar Allan Poe Award.

In movies and television, there are three ways of describing these adaptations:

A true story. This means that everything is as accurate as possible. You made nothing up. Characters, chronology, facts, are all true. For *Selma, Lord, Selma*, I wrote the teleplay based on a book which was a first-hand account of the Civil Rights Movement in Selma, Alabama, in the winter of 1965. It was filmed for *Wonderful World of Disney*, and it qualifies as "a true story." This means nearly everything happened exactly as it is depicted in the film, with the exception of some of the dialogue.

Based on a true story. This means that the script/film is very *close* to the way things happened, but some of the characters may have been combined or invented, and other things may have been re-ordered or revised for dramatic purposes. Oliver Stone's *JFK* is based on a true story. For the sake of the movie, a "Deep Throat" type of character was invented and other aspects of the story were heightened for dramatic effect. So it was indeed *based* on a true story, the Kennedy assassination. But it was not a true story, since it was not entirely accurate in its portrayal. See the difference?

Inspired by a true story. This means we got the idea from something true and then we launched our own story, most of which we made up. *Jane Doe*, as I noted above, is "Inspired by."

Do not invest a lot of time and energy in a true story to which you don't have the rights. The same holds true for adapting a short story or novel to which you don't have the rights. Never do this. It will lead to heartache and disappointment.

Adapting Your Own Novel

Some of you may have written a novel and are considering adapting it into a screenplay. If you do that and the novel is unpublished, consider sending the movie version out first, before submitting it to book publishers, as an original screenplay. Original scripts are easier to sell and seem less encumbered to the buyers. Later, if you get a movie deal, you can more easily sell the novel version.

If the adaptation is of a published novel you have written, then under the title write, "A Screenplay by Jane Doe Based on Her Novel." And in the cover letter mention the status of the rights. In other words, would the novel/screenplay be easy to purchase? Or are the book's rights tied up and will have to be separately negotiated with the publisher?

The process of adapting one's own novel is more difficult than it seems at first glance. I have known many novelists with friends who told them how visual their book was and what a great movie it would make. So they decide to write a screenplay version. It entails merciless cutting, often of things a writer has worked months or years to get exactly right. Also, a screenplay needs to find a way to externalize those feelings and thoughts that may have been deeply internal to a character. This can also be distressing to the novelist.

I have adapted many novels to screenplays, and subplots fall by the wayside like roadkill. Since they were not my pets, I didn't grieve their losses, but it's much harder for the novelists who had invested so much in them. Most novels are around 350 pages. The screenplays are 120. In other words, about two-thirds of those words have to go. Taking the axe to your own beloved words, which you've slaved over for years, is not for weaklings.

When launching a screenwriting career, scripts written from original ideas are always the safest, but we writers can't control which ideas are going to catch fire and take over our creative minds. Like falling in love, when it's great, it's out of control.

If this happens to you, and you fall in love with a true story, keep this in mind: If they're not famous and you weren't there, either negotiate for the rights, or change everything you possibly can.

PART FOUR

The Spirit

The fourth and final component is the spirit of the piece. It's time for the big picture. What am I saying in my work? What impact will it have in the world? Often, especially in the entertainment industry, this is never addressed at all. "Will it have a huge opening weekend?" is generally the only question asked. This is the time to turn your attention back to central issues such as theme and purpose. It may be that your original vision for this piece has gotten overshadowed by some other aspect. Now is the last chance to go back and strengthen the thing that made you want to write this script in the first place.

It's also time to focus on the final image or passage, where the "author's message" often resides. There is no need to be heavy-handed or preachy, but it is important to be aware and to look again. A story that your heart wanted to tell because it said, "Don't give up hope" may have developed into a story that says, "You have to be lucky," for example. It is not that difficult to go through your piece and find those places where hope should be. Protect that flickering candle flame from the winds of plot so it doesn't get blown out.

CHAPTER 27

The Truth

The most important thing in later drafts of your screenplay is to dig deeper, finding your way to the heart of the story. You need to find the truth for the characters. The truth may seem obvious or simple once it comes to light, but getting to that truth might be neither.

In first drafts we have so much work to do—structuring the story, creating the reality, setting, characters, style, mood, pace . . . all of it. It usually is not until the second draft that I have the clarity, time, and energy to seek out the gold buried in the deeper layers. If first drafts tend to be surface, splashy, or shallow, second drafts need to peel back the top layers and dig down into the darker heartland and get at the real gold: the truth.

So how do you get there? I'll give you a hint. You usually have to be willing to go through some dark, scary, or messy terrain to find the gold mine.

You have to get inside the characters. Be willing to get under their skin. When I took on the assignment of writing *I Know My First Name Is Steven*, I knew I'd have to identify with the parents who lost their little boy. My son was six at the time, and I knew it would be painfully hard, and it was. I also had to be the little boy who was lost, frightened, and sexually abused. That was harder. But by far the hardest part of the process, and one I didn't even realize I'd have to do when I took the job, was having to enter the mind of the kidnapper—the twisted, sick man who stole that child and abused him.

Why did he do it? What was he thinking and feeling? It was a dark place, but one you as the writer have to go to if you are going to tell those stories.

How do you do it? You keep asking yourself those questions: What does he want? What is she thinking? Where are they coming from? Where are we going with this? If you keep digging with these tools, and are unwilling to settle for shallow, phony answers, eventually you'll uncover the gold. The real stuff.

Going Through the Eye of the Needle

Here's an example of a powerful scene that does the work and eventually gets down to the truth in a way that is cathartic and a climactic turning point:

In *Scent of a Woman*, the scene is in a fancy hotel suite. Pacino plays an old, blind, mean Colonel whose family has hired a college boy to babysit him for the weekend so they can have a break from him. The Colonel sends the boy, played by Chris O'Donnell, out to buy him a cigar. He means to kill himself while the boy is out of the room. But halfway across the hotel lobby, the kid realizes something is wrong and races back upstairs in time to surprise Pacino with the gun to his head.

The seven-minute scene in which the kid tries to get Pacino to put the gun down is powerful. One reason it is strong is because it is one-sided. All the power is Pacino's. The kid isn't smart enough or deep enough or tough enough to prevail here. He's not even physically strong enough or brave enough. It seems hopeless. As we watch, we even begin to feel like maybe it would be better if the Colonel did end it. He begins to convince us, the audience, that maybe it is pointless to go on.

Then something powerful happens. The kid doesn't save him. Instead, the Colonel rants until he gets to the truth himself, to the deepest heart of the matter. He expresses out loud the message that killing himself would have communicated. He says, "I'm in the *dark* here." That is the truth. It's the bottom line. The thing he thought no one else could know. His curse and his secret. *His* truth. And once the truth is told, the catharsis occurs, whether he wants it to or not. It takes a few minutes for him to physically put the gun down, but once the truth is told, the bomb has been defused.

If you attempt this kind of cathartic scene, be forewarned: There is no way out but directly through the heart. If you take an audience to a place so dark that it thinks suicide may be the best answer, you had better stay in there until you pull us all out again. And not with cheap theatrics or heroics—the kid grabbing the gun—or with quick, fake answers. You have to stay with the truth every moment and walk all the way through the darkest part of the woods until you come out on the other side. This isn't for wimps. It takes courage, understanding, and heart to write like *this*.

Finding the Truth Among the Lies

A few years ago I wrote a movie for television based on the true story of Bobby McLaughlin. He was a 20-year-old kid who was convicted of a murder he had no connection to, except that he happened to have the same name as a previously convicted felon and the police made a mistake and then covered it up. He spent six years in the penitentiary before his father could get the case reopened and Bobby released from prison. The movie was called *Guilty Until Proven Innocent* and starred Brendan Fraser as Bobby and Martin Sheen as his father.

What made the story powerful, and difficult was that Bobby was a screw-up. He dropped out of high school, drank, did drugs—all the things rebellious teenage boys in Brooklyn do. So when he got arrested for shooting somebody in a drug deal gone wrong his father believed he must have done it. He thought his son was guilty.

At some point in the screenplay dramatizing this story, the father has to make a complete reversal. He has to realize he was completely wrong about his own kid. And my problem was how to write that reversal. How do you have someone make a sudden change so drastic and give the scene the emotional power it deserves? You can't just have him slap his forehead, a light bulb goes on, and he gets it. You have to design the ideas and events that actually turn him around. One part of that, I realized, could be a lie-detector test. What if the father insisted on his son taking a polygraph? So I put that in; it indicates that Bobby is telling the truth. The father is given the results which makes him feel many things: tremendously relieved his kid is innocent . . . and terribly guilty that he didn't believe him before.

How does the scene play out when the father goes to prison to see his son and tell him he knows the boy is innocent? As I said, all scenes need conflict in order to work. So a scene where the dad just walks in and says, "I'm sorry. Now I believe you," would not only lack conflict, it would also be a very short scene at a turning point where I needed a powerful dramatic interaction. This scene went through many drafts; I didn't finally get it right until we were in the middle of shooting. Here is the scene the way it was filmed:

INT. PRISON VISITING ROOM. DAY.

Harold sits waiting for Bobby when the guard brings him in. Bobby looks at his face, behind the glass barricade, trying to read the answer, and the pain he sees there makes him assume the worst. This makes Bobby furious. Before he even sits down:

> BOBBY
> Did you see the lie detector test?

> HAROLD
> Yeah.

> BOBBY
> Yeah, right. The courts don't accept them so why should you?

> HAROLD
> Sit down, would you please, Bobby?

> BOBBY
> What do you want from me? You want the truth about every lie I ever told? Fine. I dropped out of high school because they were gonna kick me out anyway. That fight at Waylen's Bar I got arrested for? I wasn't just there, I threw the first punch. I've been having sex since I was fourteen years old, but I never got nobody pregnant. I bought drugs before, but I never sold any. I stole stuff when I was a kid, candy, cigarettes, but I never robbed nobody. I never touched a gun and I sure as hell never killed nobody. I know you

```
think that I'm a loser, and maybe I
am, but I did not do this.

            HAROLD
I know you didn't. I should
have known all along. What
kind of a man is it that needs
a lie detector test to believe
in his own kid? God...I was
wrong and I'm sorry. I don't
know what else to say. We're
gonna get you out of there,
y'hear me? I promise you.
We're gonna bring you home where
you belong. Can you forgive me?
```

```
By this point Bobby is choked up and can't answer.
He nods, tears in his eyes and puts his hand up on
the glass. His dad puts his hand over it and they
look at each other.
```

As screenwriters, the thing to remember about scenes like this: They are a chance to give the actors their moments. Brendan Fraser was barely 20 when he played this role. It was his first big part. This scene gave him a chance to blow off all the anger and rage and frustration his character feels at being wrongfully imprisoned and getting no support from his father. And then it gives him the chance to shift that to an open-hearted place of forgiveness, relief, and love. It is a little emotional miracle for Bobby, and Brendan played it beautifully.

Martin Sheen's Harold had been angry at his son for the whole first half of the movie. This scene gave him the chance to completely shift gears and reverse his stubborn Irish position. And Sheen understood how hard it is for this kind of blue-collar, right-wing father to admit he is wrong and apologize. That made his action as the character powerful and moving.

It is good to have characters go through changes, come to realizations, have breakthroughs. But normally these can't believably happen in an instant. Give your characters a page or two to move through that process. Let the audience go through the changes with the characters. This will also give your actors scenes they can sink their teeth into.

Getting to the Heart of the Matter

Sometimes getting to the heart of the matter is accomplished by saying out loud the things that usually go unsaid. *Best Friends for Life* is a drama about two women in middle age who have been best friends since girlhood. (based on a novel by Shelby Hearon). They both lose their husbands in the same year and get through it largely thanks to the closeness of their relationship. Sarah (played by Linda Lavin) starts a whole new life in South Carolina, opening her own business and falling in love with an old country doctor played by Richard Farnsworth. Harriet (Gena Rowlands) is the wealthy Houston widow who finds herself alone in a huge gorgeous house, dying of cancer. After her husband was killed driving drunk, Harriet has found out he was having an affair with one of her friends. And she is estranged from her daughter, Pam, a tough young attorney who knew about the affair. By the end of her life, her best friend is all Harriet has left.

This is the final scene between them, when Sarah flies to Texas to see Harriet in the hospital.

```
INT. HARRIET'S HOSPITAL ROOM. DAY.

Sarah comes in. Harriet is in the bed, asleep, a
shadow of her old self -- pale and thin -- connected
by tubes and wires to all sorts of solutions and
monitors. As Sarah sits beside her, Harriet opens her
eyes.

                    HARRIET
          Hey.

                    SARAH
                 (smiling)
          Hey, yourself.

                    HARRIET
          Do I smell chocolate?

Sarah opens the lid of the shoebox.
```

                    SARAH
          Fresh baked triple fudge
          brownies, air mail special.

                    HARRIET
          Put 'em where I can smell them.

Sarah puts the open box near her pillow.

                    SARAH
          How you holdin' up?

                    HARRIET
          I'm still here.

Sarah is not sure whether this is the good news or
the bad news.

                    HARRIET
                 (Continuing)
          I've been thinking, when I
          get to heaven, I'm gonna kick
          Knox Calhoun in the groin.

                    SARAH
          Kick him a good one for me, too.

                    HARRIET
          I've decided to just keep the good
          times and throw away the rest...
          the best times of my life...the day
          we met at Pritchard's, my wedding,
          the day Pammy was born...I'm going
          to string them together like a
          film strip and throw away the rest.

                    SARAH
          Okay.

                    HARRIET
          I don't want to think about
          the rest...Knox and Violet...
          and Pammy...if I think about
          all that, I know my life didn't
          amount to anything. I never
          did anything...all I'll leave

behind is a closet full of
clothes and a nice house -- that
somebody'll just come along and
clean out and redecorate.

Sarah is stung by this.

> SARAH
> No. That's not true. Your
> life is more than that. I
> can't imagine what my life
> would have been like without
> you in it. If it weren't for
> you, I wouldn't be me.

> HARRIET
> I feel like that about you.

> SARAH
> When you get right down to it,
> at the end of the day, it doesn't
> matter who was successful or
> famous or who made money or who
> made partner. The only thing
> that matters is who did you love.
> It doesn't even matter, in the
> end, if they loved you back or
> if they deserved your love or even
> accepted it. Just you -- loving
> them. That's all. And you did
> beautifully. You loved your mother
> and Dad and Knox and Pammy and
> to my great fortune, me.

> HARRIET
> Yes. I did. I do.

> SARAH
> I know.

Sarah reaches out and takes Harriet's hand and
Harriet holds on tight.

Sometimes telling the truth, as simply and clearly as possible, is the best
choice you can make.

CHAPTER 28

Support Systems

If you're like most people, you have more integrity when it comes to keeping your word with other people than in keeping your promises to yourself. If you make a date to go to the movies with Tony, you show up; you don't leave him standing there. But if you make a date with your own creative self to write Monday morning from ten to noon, and other things come up, you barely hesitate. You stand yourself up. You leave your creative self just standing there cold. This is why it is often a good idea to enlist a writing buddy.

The Buddy System

I have almost no self-discipline, but I write hundreds of pages a year. One of the ways I trained myself to do this was through the Buddy System. It works particularly well if you have a friend who is also struggling to write. In the early days of my screenwriting career, I would call my Writing Buddy in the morning and say, "I need to get 10 pages done today, up to page 43. How about you?" And my W.B. would set her own target. Then around 5:00 in the afternoon, whoever hits the target first calls the other to say, "I made it. How about you?" Then you cheer for each other's victories, and buck each other up in defeat. And set new targets for tomorrow. It's amazing how much harder it is to give up and leave your desk when you know somebody is going to be asking you how many pages you wrote.

Your Writing Buddy should be someone whose respect you want to keep, someone who won't mind calling you at noon to say, "So? Did you get your two hours in?" Until you get a writing routine firmly locked into your life-style, there may be a part of your mind that will try to talk you out of writing, that will keep throwing roadblocks in your path. So get some support.

At this point in my career, I no longer use a daily writing buddy, but I have a weekly writing buddy. I call my W.B. every Monday morning at 6:30. And I set out my writing goals for the week with her, and she does the same. The next Monday we check up on each other. It doesn't matter that she is writing her Ph.D. dissertation and I'm writing this book, or a screenplay. Writers are all the same species of animal. And pages are pages. Accountability is helpful. It can make the difference between getting that script done, or letting it drag on for months.

Don't do content. Don't, however, tell your buddy the story and describe the scenes you are going to write. You are not looking for input here. You are looking for help in getting the pages written. Later, when it is written, share the details with him or her. For now, protect the sanctity of the inner working of the creative mind. Let it do its job in peace; just make sure it has the support to get the job done.

There are two kinds of writing groups: support and critique.

Critique Groups

These can be extremely useful. When I first started writing, I belonged to several critique groups. These can be powerful, potent, and sometimes dangerous things. They give you new eyes and ears to hear your words from a fresh perspective, and can offer good ideas for ways to improve, tighten, heighten, and polish your writing. And they can motivate you to finish a piece of work in time to share it with your group.

Having a group read a screenplay out loud is a valuable tool for polishing dialogue and getting a feel for pacing. If a scene just lies there, it will be painfully obvious when a small group is reading aloud. In fact, as I mentioned earlier, if the readers are not good actors, it is even better. Good actors can make mediocre lines work. But you want to fix those mediocre lines. So ordinary readers—even bad ones—are more helpful in pointing them out to you. If the line is right, it will work even if it's not read brilliantly.

There are some unwritten rules for critique groups, but personally, I feel that they should be written down and shared. Hopefully everyone has the same assumptions, but it might be good to check.

Rules for Critique Groups

1. All ideas are freely given and become the recipient's—to use or not.

2. All feedback should be constructive. The group's point of view should be to ask, "What is the writer's vision for this piece? And how can we help him/her realize that vision?" Never impose a group member's taste, style, or slant over the author's.

3. Competitiveness has no place in critique groups. I have seen groups founder when they had a darling or a star, or when one person's success was not cheered by all. In a writing group, one member's success is the group's success.

4. When someone has read or presented a piece of writing, always begin any comments with the good ones. What did you like? What worked? Then in the context of positive input, what can be improved? What is confusing or awkward?

Support Groups

This is a concept I'd like to reintroduce more widely for writers' circles. This is a group whose purpose is not to critique the content, but to give writers a sense of community, and a place to set goals. It is motivational in nature. A support group usually meets once a month. We go around the circle, and each member has a chance to share where she is now in her writing, to say what she has accomplished since the last meeting, and to set goals for the next month.

These groups are best if kept to between five and ten members, so that everyone has a good amount of time to share. We each write down our own goals *and* the other members' goals so that we can support each other. This may mean calling each other, or simply asking how chapter three is coming if we run into each other somewhere. Some members set page-count goals, or submission goals. Member A may set a goal of sending a query to ten agents; Member B will pledge to finish the second act of her script.

Do you remember those old cartoons where Pluto (Mickey Mouse's dog) would appear on someone's shoulders as a little angel and a little devil, and try to persuade the person to do good or evil? The bottom line for all writing groups is somewhat like that. They can be helpful, or the opposite.

If the message you are coming away with is in any form: "Don't write" (I can't. I'm not good enough. This will never work out for me., etc.)—well, that's the devil.

You should come away from your group feeling supported as a writer. If you don't, then you need to extricate yourself from it. Find other writers who have tastes or goals closer to your own, or who are kinder or more enthusiastic.

You should come out of your group (whether it's a support group or a critique group) feeling excited and ready to rush to the page and do your work. At the very least, you should feel challenged and yet capable of succeeding in your writing.

CHAPTER 29

Inspiration

Okay, you've come this far. You've written your screenplay, and rewritten it. You are ready to storm the walls of Hollywood. What now? I have written a whole book about this called *Selling Your Screenplay.* (The new edition from The Writer Books will be out in September 2002.) It may help you tackle the next step. But for now, here is my story. This is how I did it. Here are the ways I kept my spirits up and kept myself writing along the way.

There are probably as many ways to break into Hollywood as there are people who've done it. You don't know which brick in the wall is going to give way and let you in, so you've got to keep knocking on all of them until one does.

If you think you have to know somebody in Hollywood to break in, I am living proof that that's not the case. I grew up never having seen a movie. My granddaddies were both Nazarene preachers (akin to Southern Baptists). Movies were sinful. The first movie I ever saw was *The Sound of Music* when I was 16, and I was awestruck. Within a year I was selling popcorn at the Esquire Theater in Pasadena, sneaking in to watch every movie. A year later I was at UCLA Film School catching up on all I'd missed: Hitchcock, Capra, Sturges, Lubitsch. I devoured them all, watching dozens of movies a week.

I started writing screenplays with a passion. I graduated from college and wrote ten screenplays in the next three years, starving full-time, sleeping on my parents' couch. I was afraid that if I took a full-time job, I wouldn't fulfill my dream. I'd take office temp jobs for a few days at a time whenever I ran out of money.

The ten scripts I wrote were all feature-length and all in different genres: a science fiction script about a brain transplant, a Disney-style family comedy, a western, a love story, a wacky comedy, a drug-running movie, a murder mystery, a thriller, and a sports story. By the time I'd written the tenth script, I'd learned how to write a good screenplay—by making most of the mistakes it's possible to make. (All of which I've tried to help you avoid.)

The tenth script was called *Grand Slam*, written in the style of *The Sting*. It was the story of a young ex-con trying to break into the newspaper business by uncovering the World Series fix of 1919. Everyone who read it liked it, but I still couldn't get to first base with an agent or a producer.

In the midst of the frustration of having my best work rejected by everybody, I went to see a movie called *Hearts of the West*, set in 1915 with a young protagonist, played by Jeff Bridges. I walked out of the theater upset. I thought my script was better, but theirs got *made*. Why wouldn't anybody make *mine?*

Hearts of the West was produced by Tony Bill, who had also produced *The Sting*. There was an article in the *L.A. Times* about Tony starting a small movie company off Venice Beach. He sounded like a young maverick who was looking for talented new writers and was making classy, big-studio movies without being a big, inaccessible studio.

I called the Producers Guild and got his address. I was living in Long Beach at the time, so I gathered my courage and, script in hand, drove my '63 Volkswagen bug 45 minutes up the freeway to Venice and found the building.

Unfortunately, when I got there, it was lunchtime and nobody was around. I finally found a receptionist in a back room and gave her my script. I had no cover letter, no names to drop, nothing to draw attention to my script except the words on the page. I drove home thinking, "What the hell . . . at least I tried."

Six days later I woke up to find my VW had been stolen during the night. No insurance. No money. No car. Bummer. Then a couple of hours later the phone rang and a voice said, "This is Tony Bill. I really liked your script." *Finally!*

Inside my heart was saying, "God, if this is some kind of trade-off, you can keep my *car!*" Tony asked me to come up and meet with him. We set a date. I hung up the phone and burst into tears of joy.

After three years of hard work writing my heart out, here was the moment it was finally paying off. These words coming over the telephone line marked the beginning of a whole new life.

A few days later, after borrowing something to wear, and my mom's Chevy Nova, I met Tony Bill at his office. (It was only slightly distracting that Tony was as good-looking as the movie star he once was.) He said, "I loved your script. If I were going to shoot it, I wouldn't change a thing." He then proceeded to tell me all the reasons why he couldn't shoot it. There were no 20-year-old bankable stars. *Hearts of the West* wasn't making money. The period was too expensive. Did I know how hard it was to get cars from 1919? He owned a stable of cars from the '30s. Could we set it in 1936? I would have loved to, but no one fixed the World Series in 1936.

My heart was beginning to sink. Was this going to turn into another "you've-got-talent-kid-keep-trying" session? Then he said the magic words. "Let's do something else together." He gave me a novel he wanted adapted and said, "Read this. If you like it, maybe we'll do it." Now, think about this. What do you think the odds were that I was going to come back and say I didn't like it? That's right. Zero to none.

This job got me my agent and launched my career, even though it was never filmed. I finished writing the last draft on a Friday. By the following Monday I was writing another script for Twentieth Century Fox. And I've been making my living as a screenwriter ever since.

Ten Tips for Breaking into Screenwriting

1 Winners never quit. As Randy Newman said, "and quitters never win." The only way you'll *know* that you've failed is if you quit. I was determined to make it no matter what. I had no fall-back position. No alternatives. Hollywood or Bust.

It took me three years, ten scripts, three drafts each. That's 3600 pages, and 120 consecutive rejections. But since that first screenwriting job, I have sold 70 feature-length scripts for movies, TV movies, and miniseries, 25 of which have been filmed. If I had quit after five scripts, or after nine, my career wouldn't exist. (It doesn't take everyone this long to break in, of course. Students of mine at UCLA Film School have sold the scripts they wrote *in my class* for ungodly amounts of money.)

2 **Make it a dozen**. As I finished each script, I'd send it out to 12 different people, none of whom I knew. (Only because I didn't know anybody.) These were cold submissions to agents and producers. One cover letter said, "Dear Mr. Johnson, You went to Cornell with my friend Sheldon's father in 1949. Will you please read my script?" That director actually did and was kind enough to give feedback to a new writer. If you don't know who to send it to, proceed to #3:

3 **The list**. Sit down and don't get up until you have a list of 12 people you can send your script to. It can be someone you know, or someone a friend knows. It can be anyone who can get it sent on to someone who can help. The list of screenwriting agents is available from the Writers Guild of America. The names of producers who've made your favorite films are available at the beginning of the movie. Their addresses and phone numbers can be found through the Producers Guild of America. Then there is the Directors Guild . . . you get the idea. Don't quit until you have 12 names and addresses. Think of this as a military campaign. Think organization and strategy.

4 **Twenty things I can do to forward my screenwriting career**. These can be big or small, but get 20 things on your list. Send a script out. Make a follow-up call. Get an address from the Directors Guild, etc. Start brainstorming. Garson Kanin, a wonderful screenwriter, was the one who said, "Amateurs hope, professionals work."

5 **Fifteen minutes a day**. Use all of the time and energy you can steal from your life to devote to writing. And set aside 15 minutes a day for wheeling and dealing. If you spent 15 minutes a day, five days a week, your career would begin to build momentum.

6 Don't stop writing. The day after I sent a script out to 12 people, I would start a new script. The very next *day*. That way by the time it was rejected (or lost and forgotten) by all 12 places, I would be halfway through the next one and I'd say to myself, *this* is the one. *This* one will sell for *sure!* This kept my morale high enough to write ten in a row without selling anything. Only once did I make the mistake of waiting to see what happened with the script that was "out." It was the first script, and by the time I realized it might not sell, I was so discouraged, it was almost impossible to get my momentum cranked up again from a dead stop. Do not make the same mistake.

7 No deadlines. No alternatives. I knew writers at film school who said, "I'll try this for five years and if it doesn't work out, then I'll teach, or work in my father's used car lot, or [fill in the blank]." None of them made it. They had all programmed their subconscious minds to fail, and for that failure to take five years. To quote Springsteen, "No retreat, baby. No surrender."

8 A thousand people. I imagined that a thousand people in America started out writing screenplays when I did. Probably only half of them made it past one script. And two-thirds of those remaining quit after their first three scripts were rejected by everybody. And who was left after ten scripts and 120 rejections? Only me. I had outlasted the competition! I was now the most experienced screenwriter in America that could be hired for first-time screenwriter wages. It gave me confidence, knowing I was the best never-before-hired screenwriter of my time. So if you were wondering what the positive side to 120 rejections is, *voilà*.

9 The road to success. This road leads only to success. All you have to do is keep moving forward, one step at a time, along this road. It is not a road that leads to failure. Failures are just the potholes and rocks and dog droppings along the path. You may step in them, trip on them, or step over them, if you're lucky. When you encounter a failure, wipe off your shoe and keep moving. Don't think of success and failure as two equal possibilities.

If you keep moving forward one foot after the other on this path, eventually you will succeed. Even if you keep falling in the same direction, you'll move forward.

10 Keep your spirits up. This is the entertainment industry. Don't take it too seriously. Take it lightly! Don't let the business get you down. My motto comes from a movie (of course), Lillian Hellman's *Julia*: "Work hard. Take chances! Be very, very *bold!*"

PART FIVE

Appendices

APPENDIX A

Videos to Rent:
Great Opening Scenes

Watch these opening sequences to inspire your own great openings.

A.C.   After Credits
B.C.   Before Credits
D.C.   During Credits
I.C.   Including Credits

The numbers (minutes:seconds) indicate of the length of the section to study.

As Good As It Gets. D.C. 1:26. In less than a minute and a half, we meet "the worst man in New York City." He goes up against a lap dog and "takes" him. The irreverent, funny tone is set exactly, and the audience is hooked.

Butch Cassidy and the Sundance Kid. A.C. 6:05. Opening image: a barred window. Butch's face comes into focus under it. This image lays in the problem (can this guy stay out of prison?). He is casing a bank. This establishes several things. He is a bank robber, the brains of his outfit, chatty, affable. The tone of the movie is definitely funny. And banks have changed; they now have alarms, safes, guards. Bank robbing ain't what it used to be. Symbolically, this is the end of the Old West. Then we meet Sundance in a poker game. He is the silent one, the one with the reputation for being fast with a gun. When a gunfight over the card game seems imminent, Butch breezes in and defuses it. Their relationship is clear: They are a couple. When it's time to walk away, Butch gathers up Sundance's winnings and the Kid doesn't even glance at the money. And in a burst of gunplay, we also get to see that Sundance really is good with a gun. Six minutes in and we have the times, the guys, their relationship, the tone of the movie, and the problem. Pretty neat work here by Mr. Goldman.

Close Encounters of the Third Kind. A.C. 6:08. A Mexican desert. Something strange and mysterious is going on. A dust storm is blowing; men arriving in jeeps discover a fleet of WWII planes that went missing 50 years ago. And they are like new; they start right up. But the pilots are still missing. An old Mexican man, half his face sunburned, says in Spanish, "Last night the sun came out and sang to me." Are we hooked? You bet.

Face/Off. D.C. 2:15. A short sequence on a merry-go-round. John Travolta's character is having a sweet, fun ride with his little boy. Assassin Nicolas Cage tries to kill him, but the bullet goes right through JT and kills the child. It is clear from NC's face that he meant to kill only the man, not the child. But the stage is set for an action movie fueled by revenge. Two minutes in, and the engines are absolutely fired up.

Fallen. I.C. 8:44. A slightly longer sequence, but check it out. It is very well done. The tiny bookend sequence with the voice-over telling us about the time "I almost died" is okay. But stay with it. Once Denzel goes inside Death Row to meet with the man he put there who is about to be executed, things begin to heat up. Watch carefully as the killer is executed. Watch for the demon's P.O.V. in red/yellow strange focus shots; you can track exactly where it is by what it sees. Also note the set-up of the demon's theme song, "Time Is on My Side," by the Rolling Stones. This film achieves wonderfully scary sequences with virtually no special effects at all.

Fearless. (After Title). 6:22. Mysterious opening images. A man in a suit walks out of a cornfield holding a small child by the hand and a baby in his arms. A devastating plane wreck from which they have walked away is soon revealed.

Ghostbusters. B.C. 2:03. The library sequence. We have not yet met the "ghost-busters," but we do get the fun of meeting the ghosts and setting up the tone and the problem: Something strange is going on in New York City's public library. Who you gonna call?

Harold and Maude. I.C. 5:23. A classic opening sequence. Keep watching until the end of the scene in the drawing room.

L.A. Confidential. I.C. 4:29. This is actually two sequences. The credit sequence with Danny DeVito's voice-over sets the time, place, and tone of the picture. Pay attention. Nearly every detail works into the story. Then the first scene introduces Russell Crowe's Bud White character, who hates wife beaters. We get the guy, the violence, and the heart of this dark story. This is one of the most intelligent, well-crafted screenplays ever. For an advanced course in screenwriting, watch it several times. It is seamless and nearly flawless. It makes *The Usual Suspects* look simple (and imperfect) by comparison.

Manhattan. (No Credits). 3:44. Gorgeous black-and-white footage of New York City, under gorgeous Gershwin music and funny Woody Allen banter. This is the old Woody at his best. We realize this movie is going to be a valentine to Manhattan and a self-indulgent comedy about a novelist. Two completely different tones merrily co-existing. No small feat.

The Mission. B.C. 3:32. One of the strongest opening sequences for powerful imagery. South America, more than two hundred years ago. A missionary is tied to a cross and sent floating down the river and over a waterfall. Amazing to see. The cross falls hundreds of feet through the mists. The conflict between European-Christian conquerors and indigenous people is completely set up and in play. Elegant work. Classy and deep.

Norma Rae. D.C. 2:52. This is my favorite opening-credit sequence of all time. Images of a textile mill intercut with a photo album of Norma Rae's life. From babyhood to young motherhood. The symbolic images of the mills, the endless spools unwinding and spinning. The air thick with cotton fibers floating like snow. The factory workers, old and sickly looking. Interwoven with the young life. The photos go full circle through one generation, from Norma being a baby to having a baby of her own. And the feeling is not only that this child with light in her eyes grows up to work in this mill, but we fear the new baby in her arms will be pulled into it as well, and on and on—unless someone can break that thread. Which is, of course, what Norma Rae does when she stands up for a union and gets those same machines to stop. By the end of the opening credits, we feel almost like crying. We are emotionally invested in this character and this problem. Not bad for a couple of minutes of music and images.

Ordinary People. A.C. 5:03. It begins very slowly with images of beautiful Evanston, Illinois. It's the Beverly Hills of the Midwest; it looks perfect. Under the slow, predictable strains of Pachelbel's Canon in D, we close in on a perfect-looking school and a choir of teens practicing. And finally close in on the only one who looks like he doesn't belong here. In fact, he looks like he cut his own hair and hasn't slept in a month. Cut to him waking from a nightmare. Then to his parents watching a play, coming home. And a short scene with his dad talking about "calling that doctor." Clearly something is very wrong in this perfect-looking world. In the first five minutes, we get that this mother is detached, that the dad cares but doesn't know how to help. And this kid is in serious trouble. The exposition that the boy tried to commit suicide a month ago is gradually and subtly revealed, although never said directly. The audience has to do the work. Also notice the way the film goes from long slow scene to short abrupt scene. Varying scene lengths and pacing creates energy and interest.

Pee-wee's Big Adventure. A.C. 1:44. Pee-wee's dream sequence of winning the Tour de France—wearing his grey suit and red bowtie, riding his 1950s Schwinn, of course. In less than two minutes we get Pee-wee, his dippy world, and his love affair with his bike.

Raising Arizona. B.C. 6:06. This one is six minutes long, but in those minutes we get three prison terms, including the parole hearings, the crimes, and a romance with a lady police officer. The sequence ends with a wacky wedding. We get the main characters and the problem (can Hi stay out of prison?), delivered in a new comic tone using nearly Biblical language that no one ever tried before. Brilliant.

The Right Stuff. D.C. 3:19. Black-and-white footage of pilots and planes in the 1940s lets us know that this is a true story. The tone of the voice-over narration, however, is heroic. It speaks about the sound barrier as a demon and the test pilots that tried to break it as heroes, "and no one knew their names." It clearly lays out the exact tone—between a hero myth and a true story. By the time the film suddenly changes from black-and-white to a blaze of color (as a pilot crashes to his death in a green field), the audience is ready to go on this hero journey and believe it.

The Road Warrior. A.C. 6:12. As in *The Right Stuff*, this movie begins with stock footage and a voice-over. But this time, the footage sets up a completely fictional reality of a future world that doesn't exist. Yet the voice is of an old man telling a story of a long time ago. The voice, describing the hero, Max, speaks in a tone that lets us know it is subjective, a memory of a hero. Which means Max will prove to be bigger than life. This is a story that had been told for many, many years, and if it has gotten better and better, that's fine with us. We understand the story's terms and accept them. (The earlier you clue the audience in on the terms of your movie reality, the more easily they will buy into those terms.)

Running on Empty. A.C. 5:33. This starts out with a completely normal American kid playing baseball in a small town. Then it begins to slide into a feeling of "something is wrong with this picture." We realize fast that this is not at all the kid, or the family, we first thought it was.

Searching for Bobby Fischer. I.C. 7:00. This is a must-see opening. An elegant and eloquent piece of work, wherein symbolism abounds. The black-and-white credit sequence is the story of Bobby Fischer, bad boy of chess, first American world champion in history. By the end of the credits, the legend is told and the stage is set for the next "Bobby Fischer" to rise. We meet Josh on his seventh birthday, playing "knights" with his friends in the park. He discovers chess in a completely visual and magical way, and has to make a choice between a knight and a baseball (between chess and ordinary childhood). Keep watching until the end of the scene with his dad and the baseball mitt, as his dad tucks him in that night. We don't know until the end of that scene which choice Josh has made. The whole sequence is symbolic, a great example of "show, don't tell." In fact, the "choosing" scene between Josh and Laurence Fishburne is wordless. Study this one.

Smilla's Sense of Snow. The opening sequence of this film can't be beat for visual thrills. Somewhere in the frozen North, an Eskimo fishes through a hole in the ice as his dogs and sled lie idle nearby. A huge meteor strikes the earth in the distance, and he has to try to outrun an incredible horizontal avalanche. You have to see this one.

Terms of Endearment. I.C. 3:15. This one makes something very complex seem effortless. It shows us a very complicated woman, Aurora (Shirley MacLaine), with serious character flaws, and her unhealthy, complex relationship with her daughter. In three minutes, we realize that this neurotic woman and her little girl have already reversed roles. The child is the mother. We understand and we buy into this, agreeing to invest in this relationship, and we're off. James L. Brooks is a master. He makes brain surgery look painless.

Working Girl. I.C. 5:00. This is a good example of coming full circle. Melanie Griffith is a secretary with ambition. In the wrong hair and clothes, but with the right smarts, she is coming to work on the Staten Island Ferry, traveling from her old world to her dream world of Wall Street. We find out right away that she is in an underdog position, exploited by the men in her company, although she's smarter and harder-working than any of them. (By the end of the movie, she has come full circle, walking into those skyscrapers having beaten the game. It's a modern Cinderella story.)

APPENDIX B

Videos to Rent: Great Endings

Annie Hall. How do you wrap up a romantic comedy that doesn't work out? You can try the Woody Way.

Arlington Road. You're not paranoid—if they're really after you. A good example of a "Bad Guys Win" ending. It's chilling.

Babette's Feast. Lives are transformed, in a beautiful, uplifting manner. These cranky old codgers will never be the same. And it's shown, not told.

Bob Roberts. The subtle, ironic small-surprise ending.

Butch Cassidy and the Sundance Kid. The ultimate underdog shootout, with Butch and Sundance pitted against a few hundred Mexican soldiers. They die with their boots on. Wonderful usage of funny dialogue played over impending, certain death. A classic ending.

Dead Man Walking. Powerful images of the murderer being executed, intercut with the images of the senseless murder itself. Powerful, emotional, wordless scenes that respect the audience enough to let them decide the issues for themselves. (Oliver Stone, I hope you are taking notes.) The similarity of the lifeless bodies shown silently from above is visual poetry.

Gallipoli. One of the most devastating film endings ever. Pay attention to the set-ups. Watch how the audience is played. We expect Mel Gibson to arrive in the nick of time because that's what always happens in Hollywood movies. But this is not Hollywood; this really happened. Notice how the final image mirrors the posture of a runner crossing the tape at the end of a race. It's a shattering ending. When I saw this in the theater, the lights came up, and the audience, for a few moments, couldn't move.

Green Card. An old-fashioned farewell scene: the kiss, as tearful lovers part. But it feels fresh and touching in the hands of a master like Peter Weir.

Heaven Can Wait. All of the set-ups pay off. ("If a guy comes up to you and asks you if you want to have a cup of coffee, he might even be a quarterback. Have coffee with him.") Soul recognition. It gets to the heart of the matter.

Invasion of the Body Snatchers. The 1974 Donald Sutherland version. Another "Bad Guys Win" ending. Scary and chilling. A great button for the ultimate tale of human paranoia.

Jaws. The name of the game: When Things Can't Get Any Worse, They Get Worse. So you're a New York City cop who hates water, can't swim, and is at sea being terrorized by the biggest meanest mother shark of them all. Then your expert disappears from a mangled shark cage, presumed dead. And your shark hunter gets eaten. Your boat is sinking. Then the shark decides to come right through the window into the cabin to eat you. And as you are clinging to the mast, as it slowly sinks, he comes back for dessert? How could this get worse? Let me count the ways. The people who play this game well do great in Hollywood.

The Killing Fields. Everyone said they would never be able to use John Lennon's "Imagine" in a movie because there'd never be a movie good enough for the song. This ending gets the big prize and deserves to. Beginning with the walk alone through the woods, looking down and seeing the M.A.S.H. tents below, through the final fade, it's a tremendous movie. When these two friends and partners are reunited at the edge of the killing fields of Cambodia, they complete their relationship in the most poetically succinct interchange imaginable: "Forgive me?" "Nothing to forgive, Sydney. Nothing." It may be my favorite ending of them all.

Kramer vs. Kramer. This one wins a triple prize: for coming full circle most beautifully, for wrapping up the storyline in wonderfully few words, and for delivering a great button in the last few frames.

1) Coming full circle. At the opening, when Dustin Hoffman's character first learns his wife has left, he tries to make French toast for his little boy and it is a disaster. He burns himself and makes a huge mess of it. At the end, showing us how they are now a perfectly working father/son team, they make French toast together, without a word. It is a beautiful thing to watch. (Note: You can have a scene where they make breakfast without being obligated to show them eating breakfast. Good to know.)

2) Wrapping up in fewest words. Meryl Streep's speech to her ex, telling him that she wishes she had painted clouds in Billy's room in her apartment so he'd think he was waking up at home, closing with the news that she is not going to take him, is masterfully fresh, touching, and lean.

3) Great button. After they hug each other tearfully, Streep says she wants to go up and talk to their little boy. Hoffman suggests she go up alone. As she steps into the elevator, she tries to dry her tears and smooth her hair. She asks him,

"How do I look?" He says, "Terrific." She looks surprised and he smiles and the elevator doors slide shut. Works like a good button should to give the audience that little surge of hope at the last moment, a lift.

A Little Romance. The sad farewell ending for the young international set. Sad—but with a small, uplifting freeze frame at the end that buttons it up sweetly and leaves us with hope.

Lock, Stock and Two Smoking Barrels. One of those rare examples of "We're Not Going to Tell You What Happens" that works great! It's hilarious. This one is hard to explain, but trust me. Rent it.

Loneliness of the Long Distance Runner. A dark, 1960s gritty look at a young anti-hero, a prisoner in England, who, it turns out, can really run. When the warden begins letting him free for an hour each morning to train so he can represent the prison in a big track meet against the local college, he begins to be treated with respect. When the big race comes, he comes over the hill and up to the finish line and then stops and waits, unmoving while the warden, guards, prisoners, and crowds scream at him to cross the finish line. His final non-verbal action is a statement that loudly declares that losing is his only way of winning.

The Miracle Worker. One of the greatest cathartic, transformational endings of all time. It's right up there with the best of the classics. The pump? If you're not sure what I mean, rent it immediately. Goes from Level 0 to 3 (see the Chapter on Character Evolution, page 48) in five minutes.

The Omen. Another of the "Bad Guys Win" endings. It's scary, as it jumps straight from the climactic bullet-in-slow-motion coming out of the gun to the state funeral with two coffins. Only we don't know who's in them until the chilling reveal. Très classy for a horror film.

One Flew Over the Cuckoo's Nest. The set-up for this final moment is fairly simple. Halfway through the movie, McMurphy, angry with the guys, bets them that he can lift the marble shower fixture off its pipes. Then, using all his strength and willpower, he can't do it. He can't move it even a fraction of an inch. At the end, when the Big Chief lifts it off its base, carries it across the room, and hurls it out the window, it holds a lot of meaning: That Mac has given him, and all the guys in the ward, their power back. That the Chief is completing Mac's mission and by this act, giving life to the McMurphy legend. And that symbolically, through the Chief, they all get their freedom—even Mac. The final button is delivered by Christopher Lloyd's angry defiant gesture. There are very few movies that can't be improved in any way. This is one of them.

Places in the Heart. One of the most quietly, poetically beautiful movie endings, without dialogue. We see the town church, and the camera slowly pans down each pew, as people pass the communion tray and the organ plays. And all those who have died or been killed are restored to life. Sally Field's character passes the tray to her dead husband, and he hands it to the black boy that accidentally killed him sitting beside him and on down the line. Sweet and touching.

Say Anything. Another way to wrap up a love story. Fresh and sweet. Hopeful, yet realistic. The button is literally a "ding." Check it out. Cameron Crowe is one of our best writers of young relationships.

Sleepless in Seattle. Yes, we saw it coming miles away. That they get together is no surprise, but anticipation is what makes it all the sweeter. We wouldn't have believed a big kiss here. When he says, "We should go" and she thinks he means his son and him, then he reaches out to take her hand. . . . well, sometimes less is much more. This is one of those times.

Some Like It Hot. If you're trying to come up with a funny ending, take a look at this one. One of the great, classic, hilarious last lines on film.

Titanic. The opening images of the ship at the bottom of the ocean after nearly a hundred years seem alive with unseen ghosts trapped in the wreckage. The final image symbolically releases them all, completing the *Titanic's* last voyage and lifting them all up into a golden, glowing heaven, where all are alive again and young, and the boy she loved reaches out to take young Rose's hand and lead her up the stairs into the light. Not a perfect movie, but I wouldn't change the ending. It completes the story beautifully.

The Untouchables. After all the struggle and sacrifice to stop the world's biggest bootlegger, the last line is refreshingly truthful.

The Usual Suspects. One of the most famous surprise endings of recent years. If you are trying to engineer a big surprise ending, study this one. Not just the payoff, but how carefully the set-ups led the audience astray. The writer had the audience so busy debating is it A or not A . . . that Z never occurred to us.

The Winslow Boy. Dry wit. Very English. Subtle, classy, and low-key. But it has a button in the last line that is delightful and lifts Victorian manners into charming relationship.

Working Girl. This is one of those that come full circle, but at a whole new level, as described in Appendix A: Great Openings. At the end, instead of being a big-haired secretary, she now has one of her own, having moved successfully from one side of the desk to the other. There is a neat little surprise twist. The emotional payoff is supplied by a phone call delivering the good news to her best friend (Joan Cusack) still in the secretarial pool (giving hope to working girls everywhere), and by the ending, with the opening shot in reverse, now pulling back from the skyscraper to the same great Carly Simon song. Mike Nichols is a master. If you want to be smart, sophisticated, contemporary, and savvy, study him.

Classic Endings (Still Worth Studying)

An Affair to Remember

Camille

Casablanca

Citizen Kane

The Corn Is Green

East of Eden

From Here to Eternity

The Front Page

The Ghost and Mrs. Muir

Gone With The Wind

It's a Wonderful Life

Sunset Boulevard

APPENDIX C
Videos to Rent: Conflict, Climaxes, and Great Moments

Assassins. Master assassin Sylvester Stallone steals a cab and, driving it, manages to get hot young assassin Antonio Banderas into the back. The kid is trying to steal his career—and kill him, too. The standoff in the small, enclosed space with two deadly killers separated only by a pane of bullet-proof glass is a lot of fun.

Beautiful People. A low-budget English film that is an overlooked gem. This is the sequence I want you to watch: A young English heroin junkie with his two friends is trying to fly to Amsterdam for drugs. He is so stoned, he misses the plane, shuffling across the airport tarmac like a sleepwalker. He bumps into a loaded pallet, lies down, pulls a tarp over himself, and goes to sleep. Shortly he is falling through the air under a parachute. He wakes up as part of a U.N. emergency supply drop in the middle of the war in Bosnia. Soon he finds himself in an emergency field medic tent watching a man about to have his leg sawed off with no anesthetic. He motions for the doctor to wait, pulls out his drugs, and shoots the wounded man with heroin. The man leaves off screaming and smiles as the drug takes effect. As he drifts off, they are sawing off his leg and he is holding the hand of the young skinhead punk. It is an amazing sequence, transcending the movie form. It's an example of what you can do if you let your mind create outside the box. This is the real magic.

Fallen. I love this movie for its ability to scare the hell out of us without special effects. The rule for this particular demon is that it can move from person to person by the touch of a hand. This allows for a terrifying sequence: A young woman runs down the street in New York City while the demon moves through the crowd from person to person as each one possessed reaches out to tap the shoulder of the person ahead of them in the crowd. It creates a terrifying, demonic ripple effect. You must see this if you have any ambition to write in this genre. Beautifully done.

The Fight Club. A small, brilliant scene. Edward Norton's character sits in his office, sleep deprived, still bruised and bloody from his nocturnal hobby of bare-fisted fights. He seems barely conscious. His boss comes in to confront him with a Fight Club flyer he accidentally left in the copy machine. In about two seconds, this little gem of a scene flips around, and the power and direction of the scene are completely reversed, 180 degrees. It's a great example of what a screenwriter can do in less than two minutes with a little imagination and guts.

The Fugitive. The Train Wreck scene is the ultimate example of when things can't get any worse, they get worse. It's not bad enough that Kimball's beloved wife is brutally murdered, and that he is wrongfully convicted of it, and sentenced to be executed and slapped in irons and put on a bus to be transported to the execution site. No. There is a riot on the bus, guns go off, the bus driver is killed, and the bus rolls down an embankment onto the tracks of an oncoming train. This is a thrilling sequence. The only thing wrong with this is that it happens in Act One and it is hard to top. This movie never comes close to reaching that level of excitement again. The train wreck makes the climax, with two guys running around on the roof shooting at each other, look feeble by comparison.

Ghost. One of the most surprising Act One turning points of any movie. It's the scene that starts with a standard New York City mugging on a deserted street. Look closely at how the screenwriter tricks us, with misdirection and sound effects.

Good Will Hunting. The bar scene in which Matt Damon's character brilliantly demolishes an Ivy League frat boy with intellectual word-play. It is the ultimate "I wish I'd said" fantasy, and is probably the speech that won the boys the Oscar for best original screenplay.

The Great Santini. What starts out as an ordinary high school basketball game takes a horrifying turn as the alcoholic, mentally unstable, macho, military father of one of the players storms onto the court, screaming at his son to knock another player out of the game or he can't come home. Robert Duvall is sickeningly good as this rage-aholic. It is a simple scene, set in an ordinary setting, that once seen, is never forgotten.

Heat. A great scene that sets two of our finest dramatic actors head to head. One is a master criminal played by Robert De Niro, and the other, the cop who is after him, played by Al Pacino. It starts with the cops in unmarked cars tailing De Niro on the freeway with Pacino in a helicopter overhead, and ends after the scene in a coffee shop where they share coffee and confidences, each knowing he will eventually have to kill the other or be killed by him. Michael Mann is the best at this kind of scene.

The Insider. Michael Mann's work again. Watch the intercut phone sequence between Pacino's producer and Russell Crowe's Big Tobacco whistle-blower, after the latter has risked everything and lost it all in order to do the right thing. The interview he taped for 60 Minutes is not going to be aired. Pacino is on a beach on a forced vacation, wading into the shallow water trying to get a cell-phone signal. Crowe is locked in a hotel room across the street from the law offices hired to ruin him. It's a firecracker of a scene. It includes a remarkable dissolve from the mural on the wall to Crowe's backyard and his children playing. Suicide is never mentioned directly, but it is a scene headed that way on rails at full speed which then does a dramatic 180. Pacino's "Where are you going with this, Jeffrey?" is the indirect way of talking about suicide.

My Left Foot. The scene where Christy Brown, a small boy who is severely disabled with cerebral palsy from birth, uses his left foot to write with chalk on the floor, getting through to his family for the first time that he is not mentally handicapped, only physically. It ends with the joyous entry into the pub, his father carrying him on his shoulders to buy him a jar. "This is my son, Christy Brown, genius!"

Norma Rae. The scene where Norma Rae is being escorted out of the mill. She makes her scrawled cardboard "Union!" sign, stands up on a table, and gradually every machine shuts down. It is a pivotal scene and won Sally Field the Oscar for Best Actress. A great example of a heroic moment.

One Flew Over the Cuckoo's Nest. The World Series scene (described in Chapter 7). I strongly recommend that you rent and study this whole movie. It won the Oscars for Best Picture, Best Director, Best Actress, and Best Actor—the grand slam of Academy Awards.

Quest for Fire. The climax of the movie, as the Neanderthal-level men are taught by a more advanced Cro-Magnon woman how to make fire. Transformational. And powerful. This is a Level Zero to Level One leap, touching a part of our collective unconscious.

Scent of a Woman. The scene in the hotel suite (described in Chapter 27).

Shine. The scene is a nice restaurant. Our schizophrenic hero comes down the street in the pouring rain, shuffling and muttering to himself. He wanders in and sits down at the piano, rainwater still streaming off him. As a waitress heads over to escort him out, he launches into "Flight of the Bumblebee." The customers' and staff's shock as they realize he is a musical genius is compounded by our own delight in anticipating this moment. It is the money scene in this movie; this little gem is the crowning jewel that makes it "shine."

To Kill a Mockingbird. One of the best examples of "less is more." At the end of the trial, Atticus (Gregory Peck) has lost the case, and an innocent black man has been convicted. The courtroom empties completely, except for the gallery above, where the entire black community sits in silence and sadness. And Atticus's two young children, Scout and Jem, sit upstairs with them. As Atticus turns, defeated, and begins to walk up the aisle toward the back door, the people above him silently rise to their feet. An old black man beside Scout, a little girl of 7, says, "Stand up, Jean Louise." When she asks why, he says quietly, "Your father is passing." It is a powerful moment in its quietness. If Atticus had looked up, it would have been lessened. If they had applauded him, it would have been lessened. Anything added would have diminished the power of the moment. Do you see? Less is more.

APPENDIX D

Directors/Screenwriters
to Study

There are many people working in film today who have things to teach us. By studying videos of their films, we can learn a lot. If you want to set up a course of home-study, here are the ones I have learned the most from. The list is offered in alphabetical order.

James L. Brooks. (Writer/Director). *Terms of Endearment, Broadcast News, As Good As It Gets*

Richard Curtis. (Writer). *Four Weddings and a Funeral, Notting Hill, Bridget Jones's Diary.* Best at funny, honest contemporary British banter. Succinct. Delightful style.

William Goldman. (Writer). *Butch Cassidy, All the President's Men, Marathon Man,* etc.

Michael Mann. (Writer/Director). *Manhunter, Heat, The Last of the Mohicans, The Insider.* Mann is a master at creating underlying tension. Very stylish suspense.

Mike Nichols. (Director). *The Graduate, Catch 22, Biloxi Blues, Carnal Knowledge, Postcards From the Edge, The Gin Game, Heartburn, Regarding Henry, Working Girl, Wolf, Who's Afraid of Virginia Wolf, Silkwood, Primary Colors, Wit.* Nichols is smart. No one is better at getting subtle, richly textured performances out of actors than Mr. Nichols.

Guy Ritchie. (Writer/Director). *Lock, Stock and Two Smoking Barrels, Snatch.*

Aaron Sorkin. (Writer). *A Few Good Men, West Wing,* a master of machine-gun pacing. Nobody is better at combining smart with heart. If you thought it couldn't be done, tune into the *West Wing.*

Peter Weir. (Director/Writer). *Gallipoli, The Year of Living Dangerously, Green Card, Witness, Mosquito Coast, The Last Wave, Picnic at Hanging Rock, Fearless, Dead Poets Society.*

Resources: Organizations

Academy of Motion Picture Arts and Sciences
8949 Wilshire Blvd.
Beverly Hills, CA 90211
(310) 247-3000
www.oscar.com

Academy of Television Arts and Sciences
5220 Lankershim Blvd.
North Hollywood, CA, 91601
(818) 754-2800
www.emmys.tv

American Film Institute
2021 North Western Ave.
Hollywood, CA, 90027
(323) 856-7600
www.afionline.org

Directors Guild of America
7920 Sunset Blvd.
Los Angeles, CA, 90046
(310) 289-2000
www.dga.org

Producers Guild of America
6363 Sunset Blvd., 9th floor
Los Angeles, CA, 90028
(323) 960-2590
www.producersguild.org

Screen Actors Guild
5757 Wilshire Blvd.
Los Angeles, CA 90036-3600
(232) 954-1600
www.sag.org

Women in Film
8857 West Olympic Blvd., Suite 203
Beverly Hills, CA, 90211
(310) 657-5144
www.wif.org

Writers Guild of America
7000 W. 3rd
Los Angeles, CA, 90048
(232) 951-5144
www.wga.org

APPENDIX F
Internet Resources
for Screenwriters

Contributed by Debra Stone

Absolute Write www.absolutewrite.com
Writing website for all genres. Good articles.

Academy of Motion Picture Arts and Sciences www.oscars.org
Website of the Academy

Actors and their agents
http://modigliani.brandx.net/user/musofire/talent.csv.txt
Database of actor/actress contacts

Ain't It Cool News www.aint-it-cool-news.com
Gossip and info on upcoming movies and projects

American Film Institute www.afionline.com
Film organization website

American Zoetrope (AZ) www.zoetrope.com
Online peer review. Terrific resource for feedback/workshopping your scripts

Ask Dr. Hollywood http://home.earthlink.net/%7Edare2b/faq.htm
Question and answers from an industry pro

Atom Films www.atomfilms.com
Site for shorts

Celluloid Jungle www.celluloidjungle.com
Comprehensive screenwriting and research site

Christopher Vogler www.thewritersjourney.com
Chris Vogler's website, author of *The Writer's Journey*, adapting Joseph Campbell's concepts for screenwriters.

Cineparlance http://www.netwiz.net/~rdef/cineparlance/cineparlance.htm
Interviews with directors

Creative Screenwriting www.creativescreenwriting.com
Screenwriter magazine

Directors Guild of America www.dga.org
Directors website

Done Deal www.scriptsales.com
Script sales and marketing info

Drews Script-O-Rama www.script-o-rama.com
Scripts you can download

Fade In www.fadeinmag.com
Screenwriting magazine

Film Tracker www.filmtracker.com
Site with various industry folk networking

Film.com http://www.film.com/watch/interviews.html
Interviews and streaming video

Filmmaker www.filmmakers.com
Site about making films

Goodstory www.goodstory.com
Pay site to upload scripts—agents are referring queries here

Hollywood Book City
http://www.hollywoodbookcity.com/cgi-bin/mvscript.cgi
Order scripts online $$

Hollywood Creative Directory www.hcdonline.com
Production company and agent/manager directory $$

Hollywood Lit Sales www.hollywoodlitsales.com
Upload loglines; also a great pay site (cheap) for script sales

Hollywood Movie News www.hollywood.com
Movie news and gossip

Hollywood Net www.hollywoodnet.com
Associated with the Hollywood Film Festival

Hollywood Network http://actors.com/Buzzell/board
Screenwriting information and contact source

Hollywood Reporter www.hollywoodreporter.com
Movie and industry news and articles (free and $$)

IMDb www.imdb.com
Movie database—very comprehensive

In Hollywood www.inhollywood.com
Who's Who Directory, current projects, e-mails $$

Inside www.inside.com
Online trade magazine

International Entertainment www.medialawyer.com
Ask free entertainment questions and articles

InZide www.inzide.com
Screenwriting information and logline submission

JoBlo's Movie Scripts http://www.joblo.com/moviescripts.htm
Free online script download

Linda Seger www.lindaseger.com
Script consulting services and seminars

Movie Bytes www.moviebytes.com
Screenwriting contests and Who's Buying What (free and $$)

Movie Screenplay Links http://www.kolumbus.fi/rukkila/scripts.htm
Free online script download

New York Screenwriter www.nyscreenwriter.com
Screenwriting website

Point of View Magazine www.empire-pov.com
Articles and interviews with industry professionals

Producer Link www.producerlink.com
Producer credits, contact info, box office (free and $$)

Screenplay 451 http://www.pumpkinsoft.de/screenplay451/alpha1.htm
Free online script download

Screenplayers www.screenplayer.net
Group of writers with good articles

Screenwriters Online www.screenwriter.com
Online classes $$

Screenwriters Utopia www.screenwritersutopia.com
Screenwriting website

Script Online Ezine www.scriptmag.com/ezine_plus/
eZine

Script Shack www.scriptshack.com
Order scripts online $$

Scripterz http://chat.scripterz.org/
Online script critique group

Show Biz Data www.showbizdata.com
Database of contacts, credits, and projects $$

Simply Scripts http://simplyscripts.home.att.net/
Free online script download

Syd Field Presents www.sydfield.com/splash.htm
Syd Field's screenwriting site

The Daily Script www.dailyscript.com
Free online script download

The Source www.thesource.com
Script submissions and consultation (free and $$)

TV Writer www.tvwriter.com
Devoted to television writing

Variety www.variety.com
Movie and industry news and articles (free and $$)

Who Represents www.whorepresents.com
Check which agent reps talent/writers

Women in Film www.wif.org
Networking site promotes women in film

Wordplay www.wordplayer.com
Screenwriting site by industry pros

Writer's Digest www.writersdigest.com
Magazine for all genres

Writers Guild of America www.wga.org
Writers Guild website

Resources: Publications

Books

Zen and the Art of Writing by Ray Bradbury, 1994, Joshua Odell Editions

The Hero With a Thousand Faces, by Joseph Campbell, 1949, Princeton University Press

The Writing Life, by Annie Dillard, 1989 Harper Perennial

Screenplay, by Syd Field, 1979, Dell Trade Paperback

Wild Mind, by Natalie Goldberg, 1990, Bantam Press

Writing Down the Bones, by Natalie Goldberg, 1986, Shambhala

Adventures in the Screen Trade, by William Goldman, 1989, Warner Books

On Writing: A Memoir of the Craft, by Stephen King, 2000, Scribner

Bird by Bird, by Anne Lamott, 1994, Pantheon Books

On the Art of Writing, by Sir Arthur Quiller-Couch, 1916, Fowey Rare Books (1995 ed.)

Making a Good Script Great, by Linda Seger, 1987, Samuel French

The Writer's Journey, by Christopher Vogler, 1992, Michael Wiese Productions

Periodicals

Creative Screenwriting

Entertainment Weekly

Premiere Magazine

Scenario

Script

The Writer

Writer's Digest

Written By (Writers Guild of America)

APPENDIX H
Author's Background

Cynthia Whitcomb is also author of the companion book, *The Writer's Guide to Selling Your Screenplay* (The Writer Books, available Fall 2002; this is an updated version of *Selling Your Screenplay*, first published by Crown Publishers, Inc., in 1988). She also writes a writing column for *The Willamette Writer* (since 1995) and screenwriting columns for *Writer's Digest* magazine (since 1998).

Her teaching experience includes seven years teaching Advanced Screenwriting at UCLA Film School (1984-1991), and Advanced Screenwriting courses in Portland, Oregon, offered through the Willamette Writers organization (1996-present).

Of Cynthia's films, three are currently available for rental in video: *Buffalo Girls, Mark Twain and Me,* and *Selma, Lord, Selma.*

Major Awards

Buffalo Girls. Writer. CBS miniseries (four hours). From the novel by Larry McMurtry. Produced by Suzanne de Passe, starring Anjelica Huston, Melanie Griffith, Reba McEntire, Gabriel Byrne, Sam Elliott, Jack Palance, and Peter Coyote. Aired April 30 and May 1, 1995. *Nominated for eleven Emmy Awards including Best Miniseries.*

I Know My First Name Is Steven. Co-writer. NBC miniseries (four hours). Aired May 22 and 23, 1989. *Emmy Award nomination, best miniseries, best teleplay, 1989. Writers Guild Award Nominee, 1990.*

Sinatra (uncredited). Worked with Tina Sinatra and Mr. Sinatra for seven months. Revised William Mastrosimone's eight-hour script to five-hour shooting script. *Winner of the Emmy for Best Miniseries.*

Selma, Lord, Selma. ABC Movie of the Week (aired Martin Luther King Day, January 17, 1999). Based on the book by Sheyann Webb and Rachel West Nelson. Introduced by Coretta Scott King. *Nominated for NAACP Image Award, also for Humanitas Award.*

Mark Twain and Me. Writer. Movie for Disney Channel (December 1991). Starring Jason Robards as Mark Twain. Directed by Dan Petrie, Sr. *Winner, Emmy Award and Cable Ace Award, Best Children's Program. Humanitas Award Nominee.*

Guilty . . . Until Proven Innocent. Writer and co-producer. NBC Movie of the Week (Fall 1991). Starring Martin Sheen and Brendan Fraser. *Winner, Paul Selvin Award, also Writers Guild of America Award Nominee. Silver Nymph Award, Monaco International Television Festival, 1993.*

Leave 'Em Laughing. CBS Movie of the Week, Starring Mickey Rooney, Red Buttons, and Anne Jackson. Directed by Jackie Cooper. *Humanitas Award Nominee, 1981.*

Jane Doe. Co-writer. CBS Movie of the Week (aired March 1983). Starring Karen Valentine, William Devane, Eva Marie Saint. *Edgar Allan Poe Award Nominee, 1983.*

When You Remember Me. Co-writer. ABC Movie of the Week (aired October 7, 1990). Starring Fred Savage, Kevin Spacey, and Ellen Burstyn. *Christopher Award, Catholic Church, 1991.*

Other Credits (partial list)

A View From Saturday. Based on the 2000 Newberry Award-winning children's book by E.L. Konigsberg. Showtime movie, in development.

Best Friends for Life. Writer. CBS Movie of the Week (January 1998), starring Gena Rowlands, Linda Lavin, and Richard Farnsworth. Based on the novel *Life Estates* by Shelby Hearon.

Emma's Wish. Writer/Producer. CBS Movie of the Week (aired October 1998). Starring Joanna Kerns and Della Reese.

The Search for Grace. Executive Producer. CBS Movie of the Week (aired May 17, 1994). Starring Lisa Hartman Black and Ken Wahl.

Body of Evidence. Writer. CBS Movie of the Week (aired January 1988). Produced and directed by Roy Campanella, II. Starring Barry Bostwick and Margot Kidder.

Grace Kelly. Writer. ABC Movie of the Week (February 1983). Starring Cheryl Ladd, Lloyd Bridges, and Ian McShane.

Eleanor, First Lady of the World. Co-writer. CBS Movie of the Week (May 1982). Starring Jean Stapleton as Eleanor Roosevelt. (Jean was nominated for an Emmy Award for her performance.)

Acknowledgments

Doris S. Michaels, my book agent, for finding me, getting this book immediately, and placing it perfectly.

Dave Wirtschafter, my screenwriting agent.

Tony Bill, who gave me my first screenwriting job.

My family for a lifetime of support. My parents, David and Susanne Whitcomb. My sisters Wendy Marsh and Laura Whitcomb and my brother, Jonathan Whitcomb.

Sat-Kaur for daily support, saving me untold fortunes in therapy bills, and helping me maintain spiritual clarity in the midst of the fray.

Hilary Leach for thirty years of Best Friendship. Between us we can always find something to laugh about, even in the darkest hours.

Laura Whitcomb, delightful company, lifelong support and love, and an inspiration, always.

Ruth Maxwell, a role model and a dear, dear friend.

My Women's Writing Support Group, Leona Grieve, Linda Leslie, Kristi Negri, Cherie Walter, and Laura Whitcomb. Without our writing marathons at Cannon Beach this book would not have been finished this year.

My weekly writing support partner, Rachel Hardesty.

My assistant Kirsten Kill for helping manage the details of life so I could get the writing done. And Preston, our beloved mascot.

Writer's Digest for giving me a forum to develop some of this material as their Scripts Column. My editors there over the years, especially Katie Dumont.

Willamette Writers and its board members for giving me a writing home and family in the Pacific Northwest. The W.W. newsletter that has been a safe place to develop as a nonfiction writer. Our brilliant editor Leona Grieve.

Debra Stone for generously contributing the Internet Guide included in the appendix.

My students at UCLA and in Portland, Oregon, who have taught me so much in the process of my teaching them.

My Book Club for keeping me reading and thinking.

My dear friends Laurie Draper, Peggy Walton-Walker, Carol Marmaduke, Gail Neuberg, Pamela Smith Hill, Susan Fletcher, Debbie Stone, Elizabeth Neeld, Jane Alden, Barbara Lindsay, Sharron Pettengill, Jackie Blain, Linda Hampton, Paul Duchene, Mark Wigginton, John Vickery, and David H. Bell.

My stepson, Jake. An inspiration and a great kid.

My children Nick and Molly. You are my home, my family, and my joy. The top of my list of what makes life worth living. Thank you.

Index